D1627034

VYSTOPIA

the anguish of being vegan in a non-vegan world

Copyright © 2018 Clare Mann

First published by Communicate31 Pty Ltd
Level 26, 44 Market Street, Sydney
NSW 2000, Australia
https://communicate31.com

All rights reserved. Except as permitted under Australian Copyright
Act 1968, no part of this book may be reproduced, stored in a
retrieval system, communicated or transmitted in any form or by
any means without prior written permission. All inquires should be
made to the publisher at the address above.

ISBN: 978-0-9873461-9-3

A catalogue record for this
book is available from the
National Library of Australia

Dedication

Dedicated to all the vegans who tirelessly speak out for non-human animals whose voices have systematically been repressed, and, by making it their mission to end our speciesism, are ushering in a world it's worth belonging to.

What People are Saying

"Vystopia is a brilliant summary of the second-hand suffering endured by those with the courage to see the first-hand suffering of animals for what it is: institutionalized sadism on a global scale. We must wake up the world to its own cruelty and this book offers the roadmap."

Jane Velez-Mitchell, Author, Journalist
JaneUnChained.com

"Whether you live your life by vegan principles or you don't, given that plant-based diets have future-saving implications for our personal health, world hunger, and the ecological stability of the planet, Clare Mann's powerful book Vystopia explores the key questions of our times - including how kind, gentle people, stay sane and happy in a violent, non-vegan world - and should be read widely, especially by those in leadership positions."

Michael Klaper, M.D.
Physician, Author

"Clare helps vegans to feel unequivocally understood and validated. Sharing insightful examples from her extensive and varied professional experience, Clare offers effective tools, techniques, and resources to empower and elevate vegans in a myriad of ways. Vystopia is essential reading also for anyone wanting to break free and unchain themselves from society's mass lies, deception, and the trance of social programming, and to expand their mind and field of awareness to question everything, and gain a better understanding of how humans, society, and the world works."

Natasha & Luca "That Vegan Couple"
Social Media Influencers, Vegan Advocates
thatvegancouple.com

"This could be the 'how to' book of the 21st century. Clare Mann has identified how those suffering because of their concern for animals who endure pain can transform their anguish into meaningful action for positive change and a path to a more compassionate, caring world."

Lee Rhiannon
Greens Party Senator

"This book is ground-breaking and explains the anguish someone feels when they learn about the ubiquitous use of animals. A fabulous tool to empower animal advocates to create a kinder world for animals"

Glenys Oogjes
Executive Director - Animals Australia

"Most people think the most challenging thing about being vegan would be the food, but actually the food is easy (and delicious!). The hard part is realising how much more unnecessary violence is being inflicted on innocent beings and that when you tell people, most don't want to hear it. They definitely don't want to see it! Thankfully, Clare has put together a useful book to help us navigate through the challenges and find happiness as vegans in a not-yet vegan world"

James Aspey
Animal Rights Campaigner, Speaker

"Vystopia is an essential read for vegan sustainability and survival. Clare Mann identifies many of the cultural landmines that threaten our well being as well as our activism, and provides the insights we need to heal as well as thrive. As someone who receives pleas for help from lonely vegans in rural places, I am personally grateful to now have a book that I can recommend to them especially. For non vegans, this book promises to illuminate the reality of the vegan living in a non vegan world and dispel many of the misconceptions that may be preventing them from embracing veganism."

Robert Grillo
Author, Speaker, Director of Free from Harm

"Vystopia is a powerful and timely book, a must read for everyone. Too many are totally unaware or deliberately ignore the immense suffering humans inflict on animals. While the majority still walk in a trance, hypnotised by consensus reality, Clare stirs people's conscience to begin this gentle, yet powerful, revolution. If you think this book is just for vegans, think again."

Tao de Haas
Social Ecologist, Clinical Psychotherapist, Speaker

"A beautifully written, accessible and extensively researched book that holds up a mirror to society's often conflicted and selective compassion. For those of us who are already vegan this book provides much needed solace and inspiration. To those who have not yet made the journey this book will challenge preconceptions in an inclusive, wise, and thoughtful way. Clare's book provides incontrovertible, rational, and sensitive guidelines for helping live in a world still dominated by carnism. I long to share this book with vegans needing support and those who resist no longer contributing to the mass suffering of animals around the world. You the reader are in the most nurturing place with Vystopia. Highly recommend."

Lynda Stoner
CEO Animal Liberation NSW

"A brilliant and accessible book that not only finally names the unique experience of vegans, but also provides practical tools and resources to help us cope and get others to understand how they are being duped into supporting cruel and unethical systems."

Katrina Fox
Journalist, Author, Founder of Vegan Business Media

"Clare Mann not only masterfully describes the challenges animal advocates experience living in a non-vegan world, but also offers insights into navigating these challenges based on her extensive experience as a vegan psychologist working directly with other vegans. I can't recommend this book highly enough."

Casey Taft, Ph.D., Professor, Boston University School of Medicine, Department of Psychiatry

"Clare Mann's piercing intelligence and years of experience as a vegan psychologist has produced an excellent resource for activists (and their families and friends) everywhere. How I wish I had this book Vystopia 40 years ago when I started my activism. Now it will be my constant companion. Importantly, at a low ebb it gave me two very strong emotions. One being extremely excited and energised to be a vegan animal activist. And two, inspiring hope knowing our journey to change the world for the better is well in progress!"

Patty Mark
Animal Liberation Victoria

"Vystopia is a fundamental weapon to add to the vegan warrior's arsenal for personal and social change. Not only does Clare pull back the curtain, revealing to non-vegans the widespread corruption in the world directly contributing to the overwhelm and burnout in our vegan community, she also leaves us with tricks of the trade for strong, effective communication and tools for happy, compassionate living—an imperative step in creating the vegan utopia for which we all strive."

Christopher August & Sara Oakley
Founders - Vegan Warrior Academy & Soul in Wonder Inc.

"Vystopia is a modern masterpiece. Vegans will deeply relate to the content, non-vegans will get a precise picture of what it is like to be a vegan in a non-vegan world. This book is a beacon of hope and has the potential to bring us all together with more understanding, empathy, and caring for each other, the animals and the planet. Must read book of 2018!"

Kathy Divine
Author, Mentor & Publisher
Founder of Australian Vegans Journal

"Vystopia is a compelling read using powerful stories to convey the truth about what's going on behind closed doors. Meat eaters and non-vegan psychologists will also find it insightful and hopefully understand more about the suffering animals endure to produce our 'food' and why vegans suffer so much anguish. Vegans will most certainly be comforted by the encouraging and positive psychology of how to live in a not-yet vegan society."

Christine Townend
Founder of Animal Liberation Australia
Founder of Animals Australia (with Peter Singer)

"Vystopia perfectly describes the feeling of grief one experiences when discovering the systematised cruel treatment of animals. As I joined the animal rights movement, I realized that this trauma was very much shared among many activists. This book offers applicable solutions for living better lives ourselves and learning to be better animal advocates using more strategic approaches and by developing more effective communication skills and the blueprint for a Vegan World."

Micha Mazaheri
L214 Éthique et Animaux (http://l214.com) and Animal Testing (http://animaltesting.fr)

"Activists can be consumed and defeated by the horror of what's happening to animals at the hands of humans. Vystopia describes our plight, and a way through our anguish to make the world question our dominion over the animal kingdom".

Chris Delforce
Director of Dominion and Lucent
www.dominionmovement.com www.aussiefarms.org.au

"Fear, anxiety, and despair can overcome nearly anyone. But vegans—for whom the knowledge of how animals are abused and killed in our society can be traumatising—are often faced with these isolating experiences every day. With Vystopia, we at last have a label to describe the deep emotional and psychological pain specific to the vegan community, and Clare Mann provides a framework for tackling this existential crisis. Written in direct, no-nonsense language, this book should be read not only by vegans, but by everyone who cares about them."

Mark Hawthorne
Author of A Vegan Ethic: Embracing a Life of Compassion Toward All and Striking at the Roots: A Practical Guide to Animal Activism

"The non-vegan world can be a debilitating reality for those who have seen and cannot un-see the animal suffering it entails. Clare Mann syntheses insights from her extensive experience working with vegans and through her own personal journey to bring this compelling and timely narrative that offers powerful strategies for the already-vegan, while simultaneously opening doors to the vegan-yet-to-be."

Teya Brooks Pribac
Animal Rights Campaigner and Independent Scholar

vystopia

[vis-toh-pee-uh]

noun

1. *Existential crisis experienced by vegans, arising out of an awareness of the trance-like collusion with a dystopian world.*
2. *Awareness of the greed, ubiquitous animal exploitation, and speciesism in a modern dystopia.*

relating to an imagined place or state in which everything is unpleasant or bad

Foreword

Clare Mann's book is a timely addition to our body of knowledge of the human condition.

Each day we see more starkly the grim effects on the human psyche of our growing sense of helplessness, hopelessness and some degree of existential angst. Mental Health at long last is being taken seriously by health professionals and, to their credit, by governments.

I am particularly sensitive to the emotional condition of a rapidly growing number people who become vegans based on their ethical beliefs about animal cruelty. These intrepid souls bear the brunt of abuse, criticism, ostracization, and in many cases, violence, from those who choose to ignore (for their own self-serving reasons) the screams coming from those well concealed, ghastly gulags of despair we call slaughterhouses, fur-farms, or vivisection laboratories.

In my own journey through Joseph Conrad's "Heart of Darkness" I have learned to see these vegans in a much more heroic light.

I describe these vegans, who are in fact Animal Rights Activists, as brave, quintessential "First Responders".

Like firefighters who run into burning, high rise buildings; citizens who swim out to rescue strangers caught in a rip; ordinary Germans who hid terrified Jews from the encroaching Nazis.

This current breed of vegan-activist confronts a deeply entrenched Status Quo of vested interests and sunset industries that are grimly clinging onto sick and outdated paradigms, shady politics, backroom deals, and twitter-culture.

These activists are imprisoned in an equally insidious zeitgeist as those of their forebears. This one is funded and protected by cheaply-bought politicians, greedy profiteers and an economic marketplace where taste, fashion, and fad are merely data-points and de rigueur; where ethics come at a low price; in an economic system where cruelty is just another "externality", another "irrelevant" factor cost in the Orwellian production process.

But let us not despair. Our ranks are growing. And nature bats last.

Of this we can be sure.

A day will dawn when civilization will owe these brave "First Responders", the ethical vegans and thinkers like Clare Mann, a debt of gratitude it can never repay.

And for my own part, I look forward with great joy to the inevitable dawning of that beautiful day.

Philip Wollen OAM
Investment Banker, Philanthropist, Kindness Trust

Acknowledgements

I can't possibly name everyone who has contributed directly or indirectly to the production of this book. This is particularly because it is the result of thousands of personal discussions and client interactions as well as inspiration from everyone involved in the vegan movement. The examples in this book, however, are based on my work with clients or interactions with friends and colleagues as well as my personal experience as an ethical vegan. I am eternally grateful for the lessons that they have taught me.

I particularly want to thank my partner, Brendan Norris, for his unwavering commitment to challenge this dystopian world and create workable solutions to break us out of the trance; Sara Kidd for encouraging me to develop the concept and direction of Vystopia; my publicist Katrina Fox whose commitment to veganism is unwavering; my copywriter Mem Davis for reading early manuscripts, being creative on demand and ensuring I sleep; Demetrius Bagley for his marketing genius and big picture perspective.

Special thanks to all the reviewers for their support and being the shoulders of giants upon which I am standing. Special thanks to Nadia Perry for the cover design and Tracie O'Keefe, Kathy Divine, Ron Prasad, Philip Wollen, That Vegan Couple Natasha and Luca, David Brookes, Teja Pribac-Brookes and numerous fellow Vystopians who are the leaders in this not-yet vegan world. Immense gratitude for my fellow Sydney Cube of Truth animal rights campaigners who tirelessly campaign for the freedom of all animals. To Daz, Minka and Topi for teaching me how to be present, not sweating the small stuff and insisting on finding joy in a challenging world.

Not until every cage is empty...

Contents

Preface   1

How to Use This Book   3

Lifting the Veil on the Truth   5

Living as a Stranger in a Strange Land   21

Living in a World That Doesn't Seem to Care   41`

What Used to Work Doesn't
- Relationships With Non-Vegans   59

The Illusion of Freedom in an Unfree World   81

Creating a World to Belong To   99

What Next?   127

Resources   129

Glossary   133

References   137

Preface

Nearly a decade ago, after becoming vegan, I started speaking out for animal rights at conferences, festivals and online. The more I spoke out, the more people asked for my advice as a psychologist on how to deal with the anguish they felt knowing about cruelty to animals.

Vegans started asking their doctors to be referred to me for counselling. Many of them either refused to see non-vegan practitioners, or said their pain was undermined when they were told they had depression or that the only way to recover was not judge the world so harshly. In the last five years, GP's have referred people to me they believe are suffering from eating disorders or self-harm. After meeting these individuals, I believe many of them are being wrongly diagnosed. Instead of having psychological illnesses, they demonstrate the normal reactions of any feeling human being after discovering the cover-up of industrialised animal abuse.

I am a telling witness to the anguish of knowing about the systematised abuse of animals in society. However, my training as both a psychologist and existential psychotherapist enabled me to work through my pain and transmute my despair into powerful action for change. I needed a name for what I believe is an existential despair, and to find solutions for vegans whilst avoiding medicalisation of the condition.

Vystopia is the name I created to explain the vegan's experience, and this book provides a way for vegans to navigate their pain and become the necessary champions to create a more compassionate world. I believe it's my responsibility as an ethical vegan and health practitioner to speak out for what is right and encourage other professionals to do the same.

How to Use This Book

This book is written for the vegan who finds it difficult to get non-vegans to understand the depth of their anguish.

Chapter 1: Lifting the Veil on the Truth is an invitation to non-vegans to get a glimpse of the vegan's pain, and the difficulty they have explaining the complexity of their despair. After reading this chapter, the non-vegan will be more able to understand the philosophy of veganism and why the vegan is so passionate about it.

Subsequent chapters provide the vegan with a language and rich examples to talk about their pain, and explain how living in a non-vegan world causes them so much difficulty. Each chapter focuses on specific challenges like relationships with non-vegans, how their vystopia gets triggered, and why vegans become angry and anxious constantly asking, "What else don't we know?"

"*Vystopia: The Anguish of Being Vegan in a Non-Vegan World*" makes simple the ubiquitous nature of the vegan's anguish, and shows why veganism is the moral baseline for our society.

Chapter 6: Creating a World to Belong To provides practical solutions for vegans to work through their vystopia and become empowered to usher in a more compassionate world.

Chapter 1

Lifting the Veil on the Truth

The truth is incontrovertible.
Malice may attack it,
ignorance may deride it,
but in the end,
there it is.

– Winston Churchill

When Edward Snowden, formerly both a CIA employee and contractor for the US National Security Agency (NSA), revealed the truth about the covert, unauthorised global surveillance of people, he was quickly labelled a traitor, charged with espionage, and proclaimed a threat to US security[1]. The United States government claimed it was right in attempting to silence Snowden on the basis of national security.

People less trusting of the government's intentions saw a whistle-blower who had revealed the erosion of privacy and the potential for such information to be used by less than scrupulous bureaucrats. Further, it sent a powerful message that the state has powers it will exercise to control those who dare challenge its actions, and the public will join them in believing it's in the interests of national security.

Post Snowden's disclosure, people were left questioning the real story. Most people will look no further than the mass media, and believe the government is researching any abuses and will do the right thing by the people. Most people say things like: "If you have nothing to hide, you have nothing to fear."

This statement assumes that government bodies are impartial, seeking only to protect the public. It also ignores the influence of industries fuelled by the profit motive with little concern for people or the environment. Anyone who questions the integrity of the government in managing these forces is labelled as a conspiracy theorist, unpatriotic or foolish. History is full of examples where corruption and greed prevail over the truth. A perfect example is asbestos[2], known since the 1920's how hazardous it is to people's health. Despite this it is still in widespread use.

What is the Truth?

How can the average individual make a choice about Snowden or any other disclosure of huge proportion if they don't have access to the full information? If mass surveillance is not considered a secret program, exactly why did it take a whistle-blower to get us to question what is going on?

We cannot make decisions based on many things we hear about in the media, because we only receive information that is filtered down and understandable to the average person. If we had to research everything in our lives, we wouldn't get anything done. We have a blind trust that issues pertinent to our well-being are ethically and responsibly monitored by government or professionals. When we hear about individuals who act less than ethically, we dismiss them as a bad apple, comfortable that the individual will be dealt with and processes put in place to avoid this. For example, the doctor who kills their elderly patients, the counsellor who sleeps with a client, or the politician who sells secrets to another country are all seen as individual wrong-doers as we slavishly believe institutions have systems in place to ensure the public's interest.

Why is it that we blindly believe so much without asking more questions, particularly where it affects us personally?

The Power of Social Conditioning

Each of us is subject to conditioning from our families, cultures, workplace, and society as a whole. In the Western world, we are exposed to wider social influences as a function of the era in which we are born.

Mowat et al (2009)[3] identify three distinct eras in society over the last hundred years that have been mirrored in our education and organisational systems. The values and messages of these eras are revealed in, and reflect, expectations and ways in which people communicate and influence other people effectively.

1. **The Era of Obedience** - Spare the Rod and Spoil the Child

Formal education has been around since the early 1800s and was built around a sense of obedience. The values were: "If you don't do what you are told, you will be punished". There was little focus on developing children's abilities or acquiring knowledge. The focus was to control and get children to do as they were told. This was known as the Era of Obedience and mirrored a society that valued conformity and adherence to external rules or religious ideologies.

2. **The Era of Reward** - Do As You're Told and Your Job's for Life

Around the end of the Second World War and the Great Depression of the last century, the notion of obedience began to break down because the world was changing, and new knowledge and skills were required. Suddenly the teaching of knowledge and content became important. With this came a different regime or set of values: "Do as you are told and everything will work out". In this phase, children were encouraged to behave correctly,

7

and if they didn't they were punished. Corporal punishment was used to condition respect in children towards their elders. The message "If you do as you are told, you will get the result you need" suffused society and organisational life. For example, people believed:

- If you work hard you will have a job for life.
- Put money away and you will be safe in the future.
- Pay your taxes and the state will look after you.
- Invest in your superannuation and money will be there for you later.

3. **The Era of Respect** - Teachers and Leaders as Facilitators and Change Agents

We now live in an uncertain world with an unprecedented rate of change. We all know, although older baby boomers might prefer it were not the case, that there is no such thing as a job for life or a world that stands still. This is mirrored in changing attitudes towards systems and people who traditionally would have engendered respect purely because of their position.

Today doctors, politicians, managers, teachers and religious leaders are questioned, and ready access to information through social media allows us to become informed and to question services that were once taken for granted. This puts the onus for performance and earning respect on the individual professional; no longer can they hide behind a role or title that once demanded automatic respect.

The whole sense of respect has shifted, and the youth of today work from the perspective of "If you won't listen to me, why should I listen to you? Respect me, and I will respect you'". In a transactional sense, the interaction comes down to who gives respect in the first instance. In the Era of Reward, "respect your elders" was the prevalent value. Today, age is no longer a criterion for respect.

We are presently in transition, with the majority of school, political, and organisational systems still preferring to use an Era of Reward model that is beginning to break down. As both formal and informal leaders embrace this collaborative Era of Respect, the potential for individual and collective collaboration is enhanced. Those who wish to retain control as experts (who are above being questioned) imply that people must listen to them. Many teen-parent, organisational, and political conflicts occur because of this assumption of expertise:

- As a politician or CEO, I know best.
- As a parent, I know more than a teenager.
- As a professional I know what to do.
- I sell this product and know what you need.

Despite the growing influence of this Era of Respect and access to more information, in issues of national security or where big profits are involved, we are still unable to access the full information, hence why whistle-blowers are so important. We are also subject to the most fatal of our limitations: Wilful Ignorance.

> *Wilful Ignorance*:
> *"The practice or act of intentional and blatant avoidance, disregard or disagreement with facts, empirical evidence, and well-founded arguments because they oppose or contradict one's existing personal beliefs".*

Many people are too overwhelmed, lazy or indifferent to question things. For example, if we hear or read a report that tap water is bad for us, at face value we're unable to discern between someone informing us for our own health or the marketer set to profit from us switching to bottled water.

In an increasing complex and information-rich world, we are conditioned to be wilfully ignorant and consider issues only within a narrow bandwidth or interest. However, when we avoid matters that do influence us directly, the cost is greater. For example, the vast majority of people are wilfully ignorant in relation to issues around education, healthcare, diet, and our natural environment.

Ideas contrary to the norm are vehemently resisted, particularly those that affect us directly such as healthcare, lifestyle and diet. This is until they become the new norm. For example, many people resisted equality between the sexes, denying same-sex couples the right to marry. In 2017 the Australian public overwhelmingly agreed to recognise same-sex partnerships, paving the way to allowing same-sex marriage to become legal[4]. Many young people today don't understand their grandparent's resistance to same-sex marriage. Their elders have grown up in the Era of Respect with most believing there are more pressing issues to address. Many are unaware of the decades of campaigning for equal rights, whereas those active in it see how much society's views have changed over time.

Shifts in Collective Thinking about Health and Wellbeing

In the last decade there has been a tremendous increase in people adopting a vegetarian or vegan diet[5,6]. In Britain alone it is estimated that 542,000 people are now following a vegan diet, up from the last estimate of 150,000 people ten years earlier. Following ridicule and resistance after the Second World War, for the last quarter of the 20th century in the West, most restaurants have served a vegetarian option. In the last decade, we have seen a massive increase in the uptake of veganism, and again those early adopters have been ridiculed or seen as a threat to normal behaviour. For example, the promotional videos for the 2017/2018 Australia Day celebrations directly ridiculed vegans, pointing to their "un-Australian" behaviour for not eating meat.

Many people find it amusing to ridicule vegans because, like other socially shared experiences, they experience it within an awareness of the increase of this lifestyle choice. For the average person, this is okay until your family member says they are becoming vegan. This is no doubt similar to public dialogue about same-sex relationships. The lens on this discussion changes dramatically when someone is confronted with having to consider it within their own family dynamic.

The following example explores the impact of our individual reactions within a social context.

Story of the Abducted Child

Over the years I've heard the very unique stories of thousands of clients, and examples of how everyone faces experiences where they either "break down" or "break through". Many of those stories are harrowing, renewing my respect for people's potential to survive and break the cycle of abuse and despair. Everyone's story has affected me, but there is one I will never forget. It's about a young girl called Ellie.

Ellie was abducted from her mother shortly after her birth. She was not the first baby Ellie's mother had lost and despite how much she cried and protested, she was powerless to save her child. Ellie's mother no doubt knew the fate that her daughter would face: sexually abused and a "baby machine" for the abductors who would continue this cruel trafficking. Ellie, her mother, and sisters would never know the close bonds of family and Ellie's pain was indescribable. The only crime Ellie had committed was her gender and she was caught in a cycle of abuse with her reproductive system hijacked for profit.

As I heard Ellie's story I tried to imagine her pain and that of her mother. How would her mother have felt having carried Ellie for nine months, given birth, and then robbed of the opportunity to protect her young? Nature had prepared her body to be there for her child and her milk was ready to suckle her baby. The powerlessness, anguish and agony she would have endured is unfathomable. Ellie, too young to make sense of the situation, would have reached for her mother but be met with a barren environment, resulting in anxiety, fear and trauma.

Who is Ellie?

Ellie was in fact a young calf, taken from her mother at birth so milk meant for her could be bottled and sold for human consumption. This is standard practice in any form of dairy farm. The mother cow must give birth in order to produce milk, and calves compete with the dairy industry for cow's milk so are forcibly removed as quickly as possible, within 12 to 24 hours of being born.

Male or "bobby" calves[7] are considered the dairy industry's waste, and are killed within a few days of birth, or, if reared for veal, at 3 months old. Female calves continue the dairy industry's cycle of misery. Bobby calves are worth very little financially although their by-products (more lucrative than their meat) are exported overseas and often used for human baby food. Their fourth stomach is dried and used in the production of cheeses, including parmesan. Other parts of their bodies are used for pharmaceutical products.

A Change In Perception

What are your reactions to this story? Did your feelings change when you realised it was an animal abduction and not a human one? If this was the case, why do you think this was? For many people, their reaction changes and they feel less able to empathise with the suffering of the cow than a human. Why is this so? Is it because we have a hidden belief that animals don't suffer in the same way as humans? Or do we just not have enough capacity to extend our empathy beyond our own family, community or species? Whatever our reaction, our interpretation of events is happening with an existing personal, social and cultural value system. What else are we cutting ourselves off from that, with a different lens, we might see differently?

Story of the Aboriginal Baby

Attitudes and beliefs change over time and what is acceptable by individuals, a community or a whole society at one time is not acceptable at another. I recall a story told by a friend when I first came to Australia nearly twenty years ago that demonstrates this point.

Geoff recalled that when he was a boy, his father told him a story about the racist treatment of Aboriginal people in Australia. Aboriginals are the indigenous people of Australia who were marginalised by the white settlers who invaded over two hundred years ago. Many Aboriginals were killed in acts of genocide[8]. Geoff's grandfather said that when he was a boy, his family had little money to entertain children. Toys were a luxury, particularly in this rural family. However, on several occasions an Aboriginal baby was given to white children to amuse them. Geoff asked his grandfather what happened to the babies later. The reply was, "They were most likely drowned in a bucket!"

Whether these children were drowned or not, the reply reveals the abuse, racism and slavery these children were born into, because of the colour of their skin.

Most people are horrified when they hear this story, grateful that society's values have changed to stop such racial ignorance. However, there was a time when this was seen as acceptable – at least to the white majority of 1960s Australia.

We see a similar division of our beliefs when apportioning greater protection to some animals than others. For example, the Gadhimai festival in Nepal which sacrificed animals on a mass scale every five years. After international pressure, in 2017 the Gadhimai Temple Trust converted the festival to a celebration of life, transforming a 300 year tradition of animal cruelty[9].

Similarly, in 2017 Animals Australia uncovered the Bali Meat Trade where tourists were unwittingly eating dogs they believed to be other animals. The Balinese government banned this practice, although many tourists don't bat an eyelid at eating other animals[10].

Animals Raised for Food vs Companion Animals

History holds numerous examples of prejudiced treatment towards members of different species and races, within their wider species or culture. The following story which appeared on Facebook was shared and commented on for its ability to "break the trance" and invites us to examine our own hidden prejudices.

Example: Mistaken Identity

"I am so horrified, angry and feel sick. I have just passed a man violently hitting his dog with a stick. The dog was yelping in pain, cowering away but couldn't get free as he was tied to a fence. He had blood all over him and the more he cried out, the angrier the man got and hit him harder. Then he started to kick him violently and the dog was in agony. No-one was doing anything. I was afraid of the man but begged other people to do something but they all looked on without saying anything. It drew a large crowd but no-one was doing anything. As I got nearer and the yelps became louder, I saw things more clearly. I realised it was a baby calf and not a dog. Thank goodness! It's okay, it's not a dog but a calf".

What are your reactions to this story? How did you feel when you thought it was a dog? Did your feelings change when you learnt that it was a calf? Whether you felt differently after realising it was a farm animal or you are equally disturbed whatever animal it is, ask yourself, "What is the difference?"

When we value people differently due to their membership of a particular race, sex or age, we call these prejudices racism, sexism and ageism respectively. When we hold different values about living beings because they are non-human, this is called speciesism. Another aspect of speciesism is where we treat non-human animals from different categories inconsistently. The story of the dog and the calf highlights the differing values we might hold for companion animals versus those farmed for food or other human use. Why do we hold these values and how do they influence our consumer and lifestyle choices?

Where do Our Values About Eating Come From?

The majority of people in the world eat meat and when it comes to eating animals, our perception is shaped largely, if not entirely, by our culture. From a young age, people learn which animals are considered edible while others are seen as disgusting or inedible. Religion often dictates what animals are inappropriate and should not be eaten. Other decisions are based on tradition or social learning. The French habit of serving horse meat or snails is considered in other places as cruel or disgusting. It's rare for us to seriously question these differences beyond intrigue or interesting talking points when visiting different cultures.

Bringing our values to the dinner table

We often assume that only vegetarians and vegans bring their values to the dinner table. People may ask people why they are vegetarian and what they won't eat and accommodate them accordingly. However, when someone says they are vegan, often a huge resistance occurs. The host may not know what to cook or feels the person is being over-fussy or even judgemental about their own food choices.

However, it's not only vegans that display their values with their food choices. Most meat eaters eat pigs or cows but not dogs, and this is purely because they have a belief system when it comes to eating animals. As Melanie Joy says, "When eating animals is not a necessity, which is the case for many people in the world today, then it is a choice – and choices always stem from beliefs". The belief system about eating animals is called "Carnism"[11].

Why don't we ask more questions?

In the same way that we don't have the inclination, time, expertise or concerns to ask how mass surveillance affects us personally, we resist finding out about how our food is really produced and what happens to the living animals before they grace our plates. There can be a number of reasons for this wilful ignorance:

- Fear of discovering information that will cause us anxiety.
- Resistance to our worldview being challenged.
- Confusion as to what is true, as people with different beliefs debate the issues.

- Fear that what we discover will cause us to change our habits and lifestyle.
- Fear that others will judge us, whether we find out and make change or choose not to.

By refusing to ask questions, we allow others to choose for us. When it comes to what we eat, those "others" are part of a billion-dollar industry that work very hard to keep the truth from us. Carnism is a violent belief system. Meat cannot be produced without killing animals and in an attempt to maximise profits, animals in industrialised food production suffer the most violent treatment. Animal welfare standards[12] are minimised as animals farmed for food are considered property and don't share the same animal protection we afford our pets. The intensive conditions animals are kept in cause disease, and the high use of antibiotics and other chemicals cause harm to human health. Intensive farming practices also creates starvation[13] in certain parts of the world, as land that could be used to grow food for humans is instead used to grow food for farmed animals.

According to the United Nations, animal agriculture is one of the most significant contributors to the most serious environmental problems facing the world today, including climate change, deforestation, and fresh water depletion[14]. Further, the World Health Organisation estimated that 80% of our Western illnesses are caused by lifestyle choices. Isn't it time we started to do some more research and seek the truth about something so personal as our diet? If we don't ask questions about where our food comes from, we leave ourselves and others vulnerable to more hidden abuses, the cost of which may not be known for some time. When that cost comes, it will be too great to bear, and the damage will have already been done.

In the same way that Snowden revealed the truth of unauthorised mass surveillance of citizens around the world, so does the message of veganism highlight the truth of how animal agricultural industries are inherently cruel with damaging effects on our environment and health.

Why Are Vegans So Passionate About Their Beliefs?

Why can't the vegan just get on with their choices and let others do the same? Why do they feel compelled to change other people?

A person who becomes a vegan is displaying values well beyond what they put into their mouths. A vegan is not the same as someone who adopts a plant-based diet. Every choice a vegan makes is underpinned by a central belief that it is wrong to use and exploit animals. Thus, they take direct steps to avoid anything that causes animal harm, including what they eat, wear, products they use, entertainment and consumer goods they choose, and investments they make. The vegan has looked deeply into what happens to animals in the industrialised process and made choices not to allow their consumer choices to finance these cruel industries. They feel compelled to act to end the abuses and yet are often ridiculed as difficult, conspiracy theorists, or judgemental and bossy.

The Mental Anguish of Being Vegan in a Non-Vegan World

If you know a vegan who just can't get on with their own life and feels distressed that others, particularly those close to them, aren't vegan, it's because they are suffering from a deep existential anguish known as Vystopia.

> *Vystopia:*
>
> *The Existential crisis experienced by vegans, arising out of an awareness of the trance-like collusion with a dystopian world and the awareness of the greed, ubiquitous animal exploitation, and speciesism in a modern dystopia.*

What if these vegans are imploring us to question our world, and take more responsibility for our choices and what we allow others to do behind closed doors? If this is the case, then perhaps it's time to enter the vegan's world and find out why they find it so difficult to live in a non-vegan world.

Chapter 2

Living as a Stranger in a Strange Land

When you get a new worldview you get a new world.
It's like the shift from medieval Christianity to the Renaissance and
enlightenment.

– Barbara Marx Hubbard

Waking up in a Foreign Country

Imagine waking up in a foreign country. You're not sure how you got there but you wake up and everything is different. The road signs don't mean anything and the shops in the street are only recognisable by what they have in the windows. Other people go merrily on their way, speaking in a language you don't understand and they don't seem to notice your discomfort. Everything's familiar in one way and yet it's like being on another planet. You don't know what to do so you try to find someone who speaks your language. People either laugh at your accent and desperate attempts to be understood, or laugh at your clothes, hairstyle or outdated phone. Then you remember your phone and are relieved because "Google's Your Friend", right? The battery's flat and your charger doesn't fit in the wall plug. Now you start to get really scared. You try to buy food by pointing to what you want but the shop assistant doesn't accept the money you have in your purse.

If you've ever visited overseas, you may have felt disorientated but you can live with it because you've chosen to go on an adventure. You have your phone, a direct line to friends on social media, and most people speak English anyway. But imagine not being a traveller, nor on holiday. In a split second, you panic thinking, "Oh my god, what if I never get out of this?"

If this happened to you, what would you feel? It's likely to be:

- Isolation
- Fear
- Panic
- Despair
- Anxiety
- Desperation

And as time goes on and you're afraid you'll never see your friends and family again, your panic would increase. One day you recognise someone and rush up to them, saying, "Thank God!" only to be shrugged off and hear, "What's your problem? Do I know you?" Now your despair would turn to grief, loss, and a fear you've never felt before. The isolation and panic would be unbearable. The more you try to get people to understand you, the worse it would become as they become angry, telling you never to speak to them again. What has happened to your world?

If you can imagine this, you'll catch a glimpse of what it's like for someone who's become vegan, because for them the world they knew has become alien. If you are vegan, this experience is probably very relatable. You don't have to imagine it because you've experienced a very similar thing, possibly on a daily basis. You may be experiencing it right now and you feel this level of despair because you have discovered the enormous level of animal cruelty involved in the production of food, clothing, entertainment, cosmetic testing, household products, and more.

This experience is not the same for someone who is on a plant based diet. Whilst they might be laughed at for "fussy eating" they're not continually traumatised by the animal abuse that silently underpins our everyday lifestyles. They may not recognise other people's collusion with and refusal to talk about these issues.

Every day now, you struggle with the pain of knowing what happens to animals. Perhaps your world before was ok, with the normal ups and downs. Then one day your eyes were opened and everything changed. You no longer see meat on a plate but a living creature begging for its life. Milk and cheese bring up violent images of a mother cow bashing her head against a crate, desperately trying to reach for her newborn calf, stolen for human milk consumption. The leather couch which was comfortable before is the skin of an animal, and every time you see the hand-wash in the bathroom at work you hear rabbits screeching from the testing on their eyes[15]. The horror story continues and gets worse when other people dismiss, undermine or laugh at your sensitivity, saying, "Surely it can't be that bad? The Government would never allow it!"

Emigrating to Another Country

Very few of us would ever experience living in a different country with no contact with the outside world, but we can probably imagine it. However, a lot of people emigrate or go to live in a different part of their own country. Imagine doing this, but your friends and family refuse to visit. You tell them it's like paradise: The weather's better, the air's cleaner and the lifestyle's healthier. They make excuses for not visiting, and if you push them too hard they say: "It's not all it's cracked up to be! You'll realise that one day and want to come back". You tell them you used to feel this until you moved. Still they refuse, say it wouldn't work for them and that they're too old to change. You tell them that by staying where they were born, they're actually adding to the destruction of the planet, and behind closed doors, a lot of suffering goes into supporting their lifestyle. Now they get angry, refuse to discuss any aspect of your new life, and ban you from talking about it when you see them.

A lot of people who have physically moved experience something very similar. Perhaps this is because when you leave you're saying, "somewhere else is better". Even if you've moved for work or practical reasons, the silent message is that what you have left behind is not as good as what you have now, or else you would return. This means that others' choice to stay is not the best one, and people resist this.

As vegans, we experience something very similar when we tell our family and friends that we've become vegan. Despite the evidence of the health, environmental, animal welfare, economic, and spiritual benefits of being vegan, people still resist and many refuse to even visit our world. That is why many vegans end up feeling so lost, alone, angry, misunderstood, and often suffer from a range of mental health issues including anxiety, depression, grief and suicidal thoughts.

Feeling at Home Again

Can a vegan ever feel at home again living in a non-vegan world? My experience of working with the psychological trauma of vegans navigating this strange land, is that it's possible to create greater ease and enjoyment living alongside a non-vegan world. Vegans will never accept or be neutral to what happens to animals behind closed doors, but we can find a way out of our anxiety, grief, isolation, and despair. In fact we must, if we are to change the plight of animals and play our part in creating a more compassionate world for animals, people, and the environment.

People who migrate or move to a different part of the country, typically do things that ease their sense of isolation and disorientation. They usually:

- Create regular routines like visiting the same coffee shop or gym.
- Work out directions so key places become familiar and they know where they are.
- Get to know the locals by speaking to the barista, local shop keeper, or bus-driver.
- Find people they have things in common with through group activities such as night classes or sport clubs.
- Ask the locals about key places of interest they should visit.

The analogy of emigrating or moving to an unfamiliar place can be helpful to us as vegans if we are to survive and create a sense of stability, belonging, and connection with like-minded people. Vegans who don't make connections with people who truly understand them and avoid addressing their own pain risk becoming anxious, depressed, or suffering from more chronic forms of mental illness.

Understanding the Psychology of Vystopia

It's not only vegans who empathise deeply with the suffering of others. Many non-vegans are deeply distressed by social injustices like child slavery, treatment of refugees, and economic inequities which leave people of poorer nations without the basics of food, healthcare, and shelter. Many people might feel that the vegan's symptoms of distress must be similar to other forms of personal distress at a whole range of life's challenges. So why do vegans say that they only really feel understood by other vegans, or are often only willing to seek professional help from those who are also vegan? Why do so many vegans feel that non-vegan professionals are unable to fully help them, when the labels given to their experience are recognisable by, and the same as non-vegans, such as depression, anxiety, and grief?

Personal Insight from a Vegan Psychologist

For over twenty-five years I have worked as a psychologist in organisations, private practice, and in a voluntary capacity. I have witnessed human suffering from a wide variety of causes with symptoms including anxiety, depression, grief, relationship problems, self-harm and mood disorders. Whatever their presenting symptoms, my job is to help people identify the source of their distress, so they can go on to find better ways to live more productive lives.

Like so many vegans, my own journey started with me becoming vegetarian. Graphic footage from Animals Australia about the factory farming of pigs resulted in me becoming an ethical vegan. After seeing the treatment of pigs in intensive farming, I asked, "Why didn't I know this?" My anger and distress at what I had learnt led me to look further, and to become very outspoken as an animal rights campaigner. More and more vegans sought my services as a psychologist, saying they only felt comfortable with a vegan who they felt understood their anguish. Through these sessions, a pattern has emerged as to the nature and enormity of the typical vegan's distress.

For almost every vegan who came to see me, their symptoms were related to their eyes being opened to the systemised cruelty towards animals in our society. Their distress was compounded when they started to tell their friends and family, whom they were sure would be equally upset by it. Instead, many people responded with ridicule, criticism, and anger, saying that everyone has a right to choose what to eat. These feelings of frustration and powerlessness then often turned to complicated grief as they were unable to reconcile competing beliefs that the people they loved were capable of turning their eyes away from the suffering their consumer choices were financing. The typical symptoms they reported included:

- Complicated grief
- Mental anguish
- Depression
- Anxiety
- Self-medication
- Anger and despair
- Self-harm
- Suicidal thoughts
- Hopelessness
- Loneliness
- Post-Traumatic Stress Disorder (PTSD)

The Burden of Knowing

Like many who have made the journey before me, the discovery of systemised torture and cruelty to animals within our modern society left me horrified. I experienced similar symptoms to those of my vegan clients. Did this mean I was mentally ill, or were my responses an understandable and necessary response to the horror of the cover-up I had discovered? I believe it is the latter.

My journey into veganism arose from my eyes being suddenly opened to the large-scale abuse of animals in our industrial system[16]. It was almost impossible to take in, and undeniably one of the most painful things I have ever experienced.

The realisation that approximately 56 billion animals per year are killed for a mere 7.5 billion humans was appalling. These animals are merely cogs in the machinery of business who consider them no more than units of production and profit.

The reality I faced was indeed a dystopia, namely; "An imagined place or state in which everything is unpleasant or bad, typically a totalitarian or environmentally degraded one"[17] (Wikipedia).

However, as far as the industrial abuse of animals is concerned, this wasn't an imagined situation. It was reality, and yet the majority of society were colluding with this dystopia through their everyday consumer choices.

The more I searched, the more despairing I became. Within this was the other reality that encouraging people not to collude with the exploitation of animals was often met with ridicule, resistance, criticism, or indifference.

Cries of "It's my choice to eat what I want!" made my heart sink, realising that those who said this were in a trance-like state, with no idea of the enormity they were a part of. I couldn't escape the frequent reminders of this speciesism as I saw others eat animals or their secretions, wear animals, sit on furniture made of animal skins, use cosmetics and household products that contained animal products or were tested on them.

This collective complicity with the abuse was so startling that I felt there was no escape. It wasn't as if the pursuit of profit at any cost could be avoided by visiting or purchasing elsewhere. Even if I chose to purchase and act differently, others around me were continuing to support this dystopia. It was right in front of my eyes, and non-vegans were seemingly unaware of the depth of the deception.

After hundreds of hours of one to one sessions with vegans around the world, and further hearing about vegans' experiences at the numerous vegan events I continue to be part of, I came to believe that the vegan's pain is unique to being vegan and warrants a specific definition.

I decided that it is imperative that vegans do not become labelled as mentally ill or chronically dysfunctional, for which the only solution is medication. As a fellow sufferer of the "burden of knowing", I wanted to create a term to validate the enormity of our experience and to avoid medicalising our plight. Only then can the vegan's experience be examined from a humane perspective and solutions be found to help us. Only then can we become part of the rising tide of social action that says human superiority and animal abuse is unacceptable. I believe that this experience and associated symptoms are existential in nature. I called this existential experience, Vystopia (Mann 2017).

Client Example

When Rachel came to see me, the depth of her despair was clear from how she walked, hung her head low, and spoke about her guilt and hatred of the human race. She and her partner became vegan on the spot after listening to two prominent animal rights campaigners speak about the reality of animal factory farming. She was so horrified by what she learnt that she entered a deep depression, fuelled partly by guilt she felt for financing this industry for so long, and hatred for humans capable of abusing animals for personal profit. Her depression escalated along with the negative thoughts and nightmares of the videos she had seen.

In order to heal, she had to work through the depth of her grief, anger, guilt, and despair, and forgive herself by realising that industries perpetrating such atrocities work very hard to keep this from us. She accepted she had not ignored the facts; they were deliberately hidden from her.

Client Example Continued

By forgiving herself and adopting effective self-care strategies to sustain her whilst she shared veganism with others, she channelled her anger into positive action for animals. She applied her skills of research and writing to educate others, whilst developing compassion for those who had been equally duped. Today she's a powerful animal advocate, determined to be part of the solution. She knows her every day actions enable her to turn her vystopia into creating a better world for animals.

Vystopia and Existentialism

The Existential crisis experienced by vegans, arising out of an awareness of the trance-like collusion with a dystopian world and the awareness of the greed, ubiquitous animal exploitation, and speciesism in a modern dystopia.

An in-depth definition of the philosophy of existentialism is outside the remit of this book, but in short existentialism explains the angst a person feels when their eyes are opened to the "non-objective" nature of reality. For example, when a person experiences other cultures, they are forced to accept that social constructs like family, relationships, religion, and social practices differ based on the collective ways in which people have chosen to view them. This angst a person feels when they realise their "reality" and the world, "their world" is not fixed results in a number of reactions. They can either deny the uncertain nature of reality and try to fix it with entrenched values, religious beliefs and bigotry, or live more "authentically" knowing that we are all within co-created systems of meaning-making.

Existential philosophy can be difficult to grasp but offers a radically different perspective on who we are as individuals. In "*The Myths of Life and The Choices We Have*", (Mann, 2005) existential concepts of freedom, choice, responsibility, and anxiety are explained in a straightforward manner. You can access a free copy of this book, together with over 50 practical activities via http://lifemyths.com Having a deeper understanding of existential concepts can be helpful, but is not essential to understanding Vystopia.

Symptoms of Vystopia

Many of my clients, in addition to the symptoms they reported above, experienced:

- **Feelings of alienation from non-vegans.**
  Many vegans report feeling unable to relate to non-vegans. Even if they kept friendships with non-vegans, there was a reduction in intimacy, feeling that if their friends really understood the issues and therefore "them", they would have to be vegan.

- **Misanthropy.**
  "Misanthropy is the general hatred, dislike, distrust or contempt of the human species or human nature"[18] (Wikipedia).

  Some vegans are unable to reconcile competing feelings that their non-vegan friends and family are decent people, yet either refuse to hear about where their food came from or know and still chose to consume animals. These powerful feelings are then directed outwards towards people in general, with a hatred and disgust for what they see as selfishness and collusion with animal cruelty for nothing more inconsequential than tradition, taste-buds or convenience.

- **Guilt over past consumption of animals.**
  Many vegans report feeling a sense of guilt over eating animals before they became vegan. Some, particularly those who have personally seen inside the slaughterhouse or testing laboratory, feel compelled to watch every video about animal cruelty, saying, "My pain is nothing compared to theirs". One client reported that the pain-killer wore off during root canal surgery and the pain was excruciating. However, she didn't complain, saying to herself, "This pain is minor to what animals suffer in the abattoir. What right have I to complain?" She also went on to have the number "269" branded on her body with a hot branding iron. This marked the symbolic nature of a calf numbered 269, rescued in 2013 by anonymous activists days before his planned slaughter.[19]

  For this client, the tattoo 269 was a reminder of the ownership and abuse of farmed animals worldwide.

- **Guilt that they are not doing enough to save animals.**
  Many vegans feel guilty that their efforts to right human wrongs are inadequate. Despite spending an enormous amount of time advocating for animals, often at the detriment of their own health and well-being, they feel they are never doing enough to save the animals. This leads them to develop even deeper feelings of inadequacy, guilt and self-blame resulting for many in self-harm, depression and despair.

- **Inability to enjoy normal aspects of life.**
  Vegans report that experiences they previously found enjoyable and which enriched their lives, lost meaning upon becoming vegan. Family celebrations, holidays, sport and culture seem trivial to many vegans. From their perspective, as long as animals are suffering, time spent away from trying to relieve their suffering is both an indulgence and waste.

- **Frustration with non-vegans who don't ask more questions**
  Many vegans feel even more angst beyond telling people about the industrialised cruelty of animals. Not only are they frustrated that many people don't believe them or refuse to change, they agonise over people's lack of questioning that other things could be happening in the world which they're unaware of. The vegan implores the non-vegan to ask more questions saying, "If you aren't aware of the cover-up of animal suffering on such a grand scale, what else could be going on? Don't you want to know more?"

- **Anger with the "burden of knowing"**
  It's normal for many vegans to report feeling "utterly miserable" about their lives, other people, and everything they have previously looked forward to. They resent the "burden of knowing" saying things like, "I wish I didn't know what I now know. I have never been so unhappy!"

33

Some vegans choose to compromise their values by becoming vegetarian. This is done to try and minimise the pain of alienation from families and friends who find this a more acceptable choice. However, guilt overcomes them and they report feeling more able to live with the alienation than the guilt of buying into the cruelty.

- **Powerless when health professionals tell you "It's normal".**
Some vegans report that they feel even more traumatised after confiding in their doctors. They say that their doctors have said, "It's normal to eat animals. Meat and dairy are an important part of a healthy diet". The anguish these vegans feel is then intensified as they tell their doctor about the horror of what happens to animals in food production. When this is met with disbelief or being implored not to worry about these issues, the vegan feels powerless to respond.

On the one hand, they want support and yet they see the doctor as part of the problem. Some vegans have reported that non-vegan counsellors and psychologists tell them that their anxiety will only be relieved if they stop focusing on animal cruelty. In a handful of cases, vegans report counsellors becoming highly resistant when told, "Everyone should become vegan" with personal reactions of, "You can't tell me what to do". Counsellors are trained not to do this. I believe this breaking of professional boundaries probably highlights the counsellor being triggered by the implications for them of the material being shared.

Consistent Frustrations

All of the vegan clients I saw and continue to see, report the following:

- Disbelief at the size and extent of the systematised cruelty on a global level, much of which happens behind closed doors.
- Frustration that people don't "wake up" and ask questions about where their food comes from.
- Anger and rage when people refuse to listen to the reasons they are vegan. Such wilful ignorance only fuels their misanthropy.
- Grief and despair that they will never see a vegan world in their lifetime and animals will continue to suffer.

Client Example

Katherine struggled every day with the anguish of knowing what happens to animals behind closed doors. She believed that her actions would never be enough to end their plight or entitle her to any pleasure in life. Things she previously found enjoyable became trivial and enjoying a meal, watching a movie, or going to the beach were seen as indulgences. She said, "How can I justify having any pleasure knowing that animals suffer so much?" She felt guilty all the time and her advocacy took her to places few dare to imagine, often risking her life to capture footage of cruel practices in abattoirs, animal-testing laboratories, and animal sports.

Her vystopia was so deep she spiralled into a dark place, eating junk food, drinking too much alcohol and smoking; all forms of self-medication to assuage her pain. She realised she needed help after sleeping in her clothes and shoes for a week to ensure she could attend animal vigils at short notice.

Client Example Continued

By sharing her grief and pain and realising she risked not being able to advocate at all if her health failed, she started to make changes to her life. She still struggles to accept the good in people, but has learnt to be kinder to herself, knowing that resourcing herself enables her to be a voice for the voiceless.

Depression appears to develop in vegans I have seen who wish to return to the blissful state of "wilful ignorance". They report that they would happily return to this state but know they never can as long as animals are suffering. They know that the animals will continue to suffer if they abandon the "burden of knowing" and not take action to end their plight. As a result, their mental anguish continues with periodic respite as they hear about the growth of veganism and small wins of reduced animal suffering.

A Telling Witness to the Clients' Plight

Over the years of practicing as a psychologist, I have been able to empathise with many of my clients' experiences. Some experiences are outside my own, such as when working with victims of homicide, substance-abuse, or torture. Even in those circumstances I have been able to apply my training and experience as a human being to come alongside those people and enter their worlds. However, in hearing the stories of my vegan clients' experience, their words echo my own grief and mental anguish of knowing about the systemised animal abuse. I believe my own anguish, like theirs, is a perfectly acceptable and necessary human response. People should be outraged and pained when they discover the enormous industrial cover-up in society and complacency people have with this systemised cruelty. This view is similarly expressed by numerous vegan health professionals I have spoken with including Dr Michael Klaper of the ground-breaking documentary, "*What the Health*"[20]. Instead, until a person's eyes are opened, vegans are seen by many as judgmental and over-sensitive people who are telling others how to live their lives.

My own training and personal therapy equip me with the capacity and resources to navigate this difficult territory. However, the anguish I feel is not something I can totally overcome because of:

- Everyday reminders of the non-vegans' collusion with industrialised cruelty though their consumer choices.
- My desire to end the cruelty and usher in a vegan world, so people are no longer part of a hidden system of abuse that tortures animals, and destroys the planet along with the physical and spiritual health of human beings.

The Shared Experience of Vystopia

Existential theory highlights the personal journeys we all experience in discovering or creating meaning in our lives. I believe the over-arching reality of vystopia inhibits vegans adopting more individual forms of distraction or meaning-making. Instead vystopia becomes a reality shared amongst vegans who can't escape everyday reminders of the dystopian world and society's unwitting collusion with animal cruelty.

Apart from individuals who deliberately choose to abuse animals, most non-vegans unwittingly collude with cruelty, until the vegan advises them of it. Imagine the vegan talks to a person about these issues, and yet they don't become vegan. This leads the vegan to believe that the other person either agrees with the cruelty, disbelieves what is happening, or is indifferent to it. Either way, the vegan knows that the non-vegan now has the knowledge but chooses to continue with the collusion. This is why so many vegans say that their friends or family don't understand them. It's because they believe non-vegans demonstrate that:

- Cruelty and animal exploitation is acceptable, or,
- They do not wish to or are unable to empathise with the vegan's trauma, or,
- They do not believe that animal cruelty is as far-reaching as the vegan reports.

The vegan is continually faced with living as a stranger in a strange land, looking for ways to get non-vegans to see the truth. Their pain is so great that they find it hard to marshal their thoughts and communicate effectively. This leads to self-blame, powerlessness and misanthropy. Only by working through their own grief, extending their compassion to humans duped by the social trance, and becoming influential communicators can they learn to live with vystopia.

Misdiagnosis of the Vegan's Condition

In the past few years, doctors have referred patients to me they believe have mental health symptoms of eating disorders and self-harm. It is my opinion that vegans referred to me with these symptoms do not suffer from traditional eating or self-harm disorders.

My past experience working in a psychiatric teaching hospital in the UK revealed that clients with these conditions are often deeply unaware of the reasons influencing their symptoms. Their symptoms become an outward sign of hidden or unconscious distress which is too painful to confront directly. The vegans sent to me are deeply distressed, and say it's because of the horror they've witnessed or now know about in the animal industries.

I discover that vegan clients diagnosed as having self-harm tendencies report regularly viewing graphic videos of animal abuse, which they say is because they feel guilty if they don't know about all aspects of the animal's suffering. It's only by knowing all the details, that they can be informed and act to change it.

Vegan clients who have told their doctors they "can't eat around people who are consuming animals" are referred as having eating disorders. This is despite not having any of the typical medical symptoms of eating disorders. Whilst it is possible for vegans, like anyone else, to suffer from eating disorders or self-harm, I believe that many clients have been misdiagnosed. For many, their symptoms are indicative of a normal, feeling human's way of dealing with vystopia.

The Extent of Vystopia Beyond Animal Cruelty

One of the symptoms vegans present with influenced the definition of Vystopia, namely, "The trance-like collusion with a dystopian world". Many people prior to (and some after) becoming vegan are very concerned about wider social justice and environmental issues and tend, but not necessarily, to have left-wing political views. They are very concerned about the power of the corporations to influence government and pursue profit without responsibility. They see the detrimental effects of corporate and individual greed on the suffering of people and the environment. Upon becoming vegan, they are forced to concede that there was an enormous secret that was held from them: unwitting consumer collaboration with systemised animal cruelty. They are forced to answer the question, "What else don't I know?" It's the unbridled greed and corruption by institutions we believe have our best interests at heart that reveals a dystopian world. An example of this is the corporate sponsorship of health advisory bodies in the USA, revealed in documentaries such as "*What the Health*". In the book "*CSIRO Perfidy: The truth about CSIRO's bestselling, 'scientifically proven' diet, and its cancer causing central ingredient*" (Russell 2009)[21], similar corruption is highlighted in Australia. The wider context within which animal cruelty occurs is explored in greater detail in Chapter 5.

In the next chapter, we examine the ubiquitous nature of vystopia and how it is triggered every day for the vegan.

Chapter 3

Living in a World That Doesn't Seem to Care

When the suffering of another creature causes you to feel pain,
do not submit to the initial desire to flee from the suffering one,
but on the contrary, come closer,
as close as you can to him who suffers,
and try to help him.

– Leo Tolstoy

Question: How do you know someone is a vegan?

Answer: They'll tell you!

Why are vegans so difficult, especially when other people go out of their way to cater to their dietary choices? When someone has made a lot of effort to accommodate the vegan, why are so many vegans unhappy and won't just get on with their meal and leave others to theirs? Are they just zealots who want everyone to change and be like them? Are they so intolerant of other people's choices, that they can't let things rest and have to make a big deal about things? Have they joined a vegan mafia and become so radicalised that they want everyone to think and feel how they do? Aren't they just selfish, wanting it all to be about them? Why can't they just leave people to their own choices?

Vegetarians Are So Much Nicer Than Vegans

Most vegetarians and those on a plant-based diet seem perfectly at ease around others without having to convert them. Vegans, on the other hand just can't keep quiet about what other people are doing.

Like many vegans, I was a vegetarian and for years was perfectly comfortable eating around others as long as there was a suitable meal option. Despite no longer eating meat since the late 1970's, since discovering what happened in abattoirs, I didn't look further at that stage. When I removed dairy from my diet because of an eczema reaction, no-one questioned my choices, nor did I feel the need to implore them to do the same. What changed when I became vegan? Suddenly I was no longer comfortable being around people eating any animal products and then it got worse, with a strong visceral reaction to any situation where I encountered animal use. Did I become an intolerant, opinionated individual wanting the world to follow or did something else happen to me?

If you are a vegan reading this, you probably understand. I know vegans who have been reduced to tears at the arrival of the family roast dinner and called selfish and difficult because they spoil the dinner for everyone else. All of these vegans, including myself, want to scream out, "It's not about me!" So, if it's not about the vegan's choice or desire to control others, what is the problem?

The Vegan's Dilemma

It's only possible to understand what seems on the surface an unreasonable response, if we look at what it really means to be vegan.

Veganism is the philosophy of the non-use and non-exploitation of animals. It infuses every aspect of the vegan's life because of the ubiquitous nature of animal abuse in our society. Examples of how far reaching this is will be explained later in this chapter when we explore the typical triggers that upset the vegan.   The vegetarian or person on a plant-based diet may be totally unaware, wilfully ignorant, believe a vegan diet is extreme or nutritionally deficient, or insufficiently concerned about animal use to become vegan. Interestingly, some vegans may like the taste of animal products, but would never knowingly engage in any action that would cause animals harm.

The understandable response of the non-vegan who hasn't yet made the emotional or ethical connection with animal abuse, is to say things like, "Don't tell me what to do! What I put into my mouth is my choice".

The following example might highlight why the vegan is saying, "It's not okay to eat animals".

Example

I recently saw a woman park her car and walk around to the passenger side whilst smoking a cigarette. It didn't have much of an effect on me until she opened the back door and was joined by a young toddler. She locked the car and waited in the shade to finish her cigarette before entering the shop. She obviously knew she couldn't enter the shop with a cigarette but had subjected the child to the smoke whilst in the car. I was horrified that the child had no choice in the matter, was exposed to the damaging effects of the smoke, and was becoming subject to powerful conditioning that would no doubt influence her future choices.

What is your reaction to this example? Like me, you may be disgusted that the child's health was being compromised by inhaling the smoke. It's more likely that you would be concerned about the mother's behaviour if you are a doctor, or have a specific concern or interest about smoking.

This example highlights the difference between an action that only affects the person doing it, and the harm caused by such an action to another who has no choice in what happens to them. In the above example, the child had no choice and the mother did. If you can grasp this, you can see the source of the vegan's anguish. This issue around choice extends to any animal use, including food, clothing, cosmetics, household products, furniture, entertainment, military training, animal testing, and more.

In terms of food choices, the choice to eat animal products is, as explained in an earlier chapter, called Carnism. It is a belief system which results in animals being murdered and suffering enormously in the process. Like the child subject to passive smoking, animals have no say whatsoever as to how their bodies, reproductive systems, or offspring are used for human entertainment and convenience. This is because humans decide that they are superior and that animals are their property. Think about it for a moment, isn't this just another human superiority similar to racism, sexism and ageism?

Despite any claims of the merits of humane farming, there is no such thing as humane when it comes to using animals against their will. As Gary Francione says, "It all involves taking the life of an innocent being for the sake of palate pleasure"[22].

Ample evidence exists to show that the use of animals for human purposes is a violent and unnecessary process which is largely hidden from the consumer – until the vegan points it out. See the Resources section for a list of resources to explore this further.

The vegan has become aware of the inherent suffering of animals at the hands of humans and choosing to be vegan is, for them, the moral baseline for animal equality. As the public have been duped into believing that animals are there for us rather than to live their own lives, or that it's ok to use them if they do not suffer unnecessarily, the pain of the vegan is that of the animal and so they feel compelled to speak out to end the suffering.

The Extent of the Vegan's Anguish

It's not just eating that causes the vegan anguish. The following list comprises typical triggers that reduce the vegan to tears. I am a telling witness to this reality and this list, whilst not exhaustive, throws light on why it is so difficult to live as a vegan in a non-vegan world when one's anguish is continually triggered.

1. Eating with Non-Vegans

Most vegans feel deep torment when in the presence of other people eating animals. In the 2018 online vystopia survey[23], the biggest challenge for vegans was being around others eating animal products. The vegan doesn't see people eating food. They see the horror of the slaughterhouse instead of steak, a mother cow grieving for her lost calf instead of the milk or cheese, and instead of pork, pigs incarcerated in pens the size of their own bodies. As the other person puts that animal into their mouth, the vegan feels their family are being eaten, and their heart breaks a little bit more.

2. Traditional Celebrations

Celebrations like Thanksgiving in the USA, Melbourne Cup horse race in Australia, The Chinese Yulin Dog Festival, the end of Ramadan, Christmas, and Easter are particularly provocative for vegans. Eating is at the centre of these events, but the collective celebrations and enjoyment associated with the animal suffering adds more challenge. For example:

- The USA tradition of "Pardoning a Turkey" where the President spares one turkey her/his life, sickens the vegan who sees implicit agreement that these animals would prefer to live.

- The meat industry advertising that "Real Australians Eat Lamb"[24] on Australia Day ignores the hidden horror story. The increased animal suffering resulting from accelerated production lines is kept from the public eye, adding to vegan's outrage.

3. Animals as Sport

Events involving animal use for betting and entertainment are particularly provocative for vegans. Circuses, greyhound racing, dog-fighting, hunting, fishing, duck-shooting, bull-fighting, and rodeos leave the vegan in despair. The media and social focus is often on human disappointment when the outcomes of these events don't go as planned. For example, the:

- Horse-race postponed because of bad weather.

- Recreational fisher's enjoyment spoilt by "the fish that got away".

- Sadness of the child who didn't get an elephant ride at the circus.

- Crowd that "booed" as the matador was stopped from spearing the bull.

- Owner's lost winnings when their greyhound broke a leg and lost the race.

- Revellers' bad wardrobe choices rather than the crippled horse at the race.

4. Stories with Animals as Collateral Damage

Media stories often ignore animal suffering and point to material damage and financial cost to businesses involving animals. For example:

- Fighting uncontrollable fires in the abattoir.

- Over-turned cattle truck en route to the abattoir.

- Fishing quotas being broken with unfair advantage to some.

- Justified wildlife culls because of the spread of disease.

- Job losses in industries based on animal suffering.

- Export reductions due to an outbreak of disease in farming.

The vegan not only sees the animal suffering but priority and slave-like adherence to profiteering and human benefit at any cost in a modern dystopia.

5. Fashion, Makeup and Furnishings

The latest trends in fashion and makeup often involve hidden animal abuse. Non-vegans often believe it's products like fur or animal skins vegans don't like. However, the vegan knows about animal suffering in the more typical industries, much of which is hidden from consumers' eyes. The average person doesn't consider where their leather shoes, bags, or lounges come from, or may even think of them as solving a waste issue from the food industry. The vegan sees a cow hung upside-down, stripped of her/his skin whilst possibly still conscious, the baby calf slaughtered to make the softest of leather gloves, or the makeup that's been tested on animals. Behind every animal product is a tale of suffering which industries work very hard at to keep from the public.

6. Supermarkets and Shopping Malls

Passing food counters containing animal products is enormously distressing for vegans. Marketing displays that encourage people to eat meat for protein, drink milk for strong bones, fish for "brain-food" and eggs which "set you up for the day" arouse anger in vegans who know the truth behind the message. The vegan sees animal abuse at every turn. Lies promulgated by marketers dupe the public into believing these messages, without disclosing the full facts about health dangers related to consuming animal products. Attempts by marketers to assuage any consumer guilt about animal welfare or their family's health are met with dismay by vegans. Statements like, "free-range eggs", "stall-free pork" or "grass-fed cows" can make a vegan never want to go to the supermarket again. The smell of food outlets serving animal products makes some vegans nauseous and others consumed with sadness.

7. Hotels and Accommodation

Staying in hotels can be frustrating and upsetting to vegans. Apart from the paucity of food available to eat, seeing what even the non-vegan might view as over-indulgence and wastage in the restaurant is demoralising. "High end" dining to non-vegans invariably involves eating animals, and taps into feelings of misanthropy, particularly where people don't eat their whole meal in the interests of their waistlines or satiation. Non-vegan accomodation often also sport wool carpets and blankets or furnishings containing animals horns or skins. Images of sheep brutally shorn for profit, or orangutans losing their natural habit for these indulgences hurt vegans in ways no words can describe.

8. Gifts and Vouchers

Gifts from family, clients or employers can be challenging. Typical gifts including chocolates, wine, or toiletries are generally not vegan. This causes difficulty for the vegan who doesn't want to appear ungrateful to someone for the effort, or doesn't want to be judged as difficult or impossible to please. It's rare for commercial gift cards to restaurants, bars and cafes to either be at vegan establishments or even offer vegan options making it difficult for vegans travelling for business or needing to entertain clients.

9. Economic Growth Involving Animals

Governments or businesses that celebrate the growth of industries built on the backs of animal suffering cause alarm for vegans. In Australia for instance, media reports of increased live animal export to new markets distresses the vegan for a number of reasons[25]. Firstly, they know of the unfathomable fear and pain animals suffer on long road or sea trips. They know welfare standards favour business, with animals being denied water or food for very long periods. They know animal welfare standards are minimal in most overseas destinations, although governments boast of being able to prosecute any breaches. They then must face being resisted or being told they are insensitive to the "creation of jobs for decent people" by others who don't know the truth.

10. Culling of Animals Deemed a Nuisance

When governments report culling animals[26] in the interest of safety, human convenience, or damage to crops, vegans wonder if they will ever see a vegan world. Discussions with people who don't understand the animal suffering or incorrect data gathering, point to the propaganda people accept that culling is the last option. Attempts to get people to see facts that contradict the media hype are often met with raised eyebrows and, "Here we go again. Vegans being naïve and only focusing on animals".

11. Euthanising Companion Animals Due to Over-Supply

Vegans have a deep-seated belief that animals have rights to live their own lives and are not here for human use, entertainment or convenience. When they see "designer" dogs and cats petted with glee by people who often only want this breed of animal, they see the darkness behind the veil. That veil is the oversupply of puppies and kittens bred in illegal farms which cause mothers and their offspring extreme suffering. The vegan also sees humans ignoring the adoption of animals who may need extra care because of previous abuse, or the euthanising of older animals who have gone past their sellable dates. This leads to anger and resentment of people who further describe themselves as "owners" when vegans know animals should never be considered property.

12. Killing of Colony and Feral Animals Deemed a Problem to Humans

When governments or local communities justify killing animals because they are "surplus to requirement, cause human inconvenience, ruin the environment or spread disease" vegans feel anger and despair. Not only do they see human superiority over animals but often know about the human influences that have caused these problems. For example:

• Over-breeding of domestic animals in puppy farms[27].
• Preferences for "designer" dogs over older or rescue animals.
• Large-scale industrialised agriculture promoting monoculture that invites "pests"[28].

- Intensive farming practices with agricultural run-off spreading disease.
- Support for sports like hunting or shooting as part of local or national cultures.

Vegans also see how political spin or media arguments for culling or euthanising are quickly accepted by the public, without people asking further questions.

13. Workplace Celebrations Involving Food

Many workplaces accommodate staff who have different religious practices, dietary intolerances, or allergies and appropriate food is provided without discussion such as gluten, nut, or dairy-free. However, vegans report that their choices are often ridiculed or ignored. Vegans are often told that they are difficult, and experience little attempt to accommodate them. For example, one client told me that she was given lettuce, tomato and cucumber slices for every meal provided at a work-place team-building day despite great efforts being taken to cater for the non-vegans. Another client had to bring her own food to an off-site training day because the chef they used refused to provide vegan options. Such experiences can be enormously challenging for vegans, many of whom have to moderate their responses within the power-differentials of their job and role.

14. Glamour Products or Services Abusing Animals

Product marketing often involves animal abuse which non-vegans are blissfully unaware of. For example, using baby animals to indicate vulnerability or cuteness is enormously distressing to animals taken out of their natural environment. Use of exotic animals to indicate freedom, power, or sovereignty for "haute couture", expensive wine, or luxury cars hides the exploitation of these animals. The vegan's pain is exacerbated by the promotion of such luxury lifestyles which they know are often linked to further environmental and human abuses.

15. Vegetarians Who Argue Their Choices are Ethical

Many people choose to be vegetarian for health reasons or because they no longer want to be part of cruel practices in the meat, fish and poultry industries. Many genuinely believe they are no longer complicit in the cruelty until the vegan points out that this is not so. Like myself, many vegans were vegetarian before becoming vegan. When people learn about the horrific animal cruelty in the egg and dairy industries, many become vegan, knowing that vegetarianism is totally inadequate if they truly believe that animal exploitation is wrong. Vegans are deeply pained by people whose non-meat eating is to avoid animal abuse, but who refuse to listen to how their vegetarian practices perpetuate it.

Whilst this list is not exhaustive, it throws light on how a vegan's vystopia is triggered by everyday experiences of living in a non-vegan world. The vegan's anguish is intensified when they are confronted with arguments that:

- Justify animal testing for human benefit.
- Portray animals as unintelligent or non-sentient.
- Justify insufficient penalties for animal neglect or abuse.
- Deem animal suffering as inconsequential next to human suffering.
- Argue that animals are of less value than humans.

Client Example

When Susan came to see me, although unhappy her parents weren't vegan she believed that repeated exposure to the cover-up about animal cruelty would result in them making the change. Her parents had adopted a plant-based diet for health reasons, but she wanted them to become vegan based on values of social justice, not personal preference. She felt the frustration many animal advocates feel when people become either vegetarian or plant-based to meet their own needs without any reference to animal rights. Vegans report similar things when someone becomes vegetarian saying they are against animal cruelty but then refuse to hear about the eggs or dairy industries.

Susan's despair grew when her parents changed their diet but resisted questioning other things society holds to be true. Her parents called her a conspiracy theorist when she questioned everything, telling them that if we didn't know about the cover-up of animal abuse, how can we believe anything without further investigation. She felt alone when they called her negative for questioning the integrity of the government, medicine, education or interpretations of media exposes like bombings or security breaches.

Susan, like many animal advocates experience a deep sense of loss in the intimacy of relationships with people who don't share their passion for questioning everything, having found about such a cover up in animal use. In our sessions, Susan worked through her grief and anger and by improving her communication, found creative ways to get people to question more things. I believe that when vegans see themselves as thought leaders skilfully opening people up to question how the world is, they play a powerful role in ushering in a better world – for animals, people and the planet.

Typical Responses by Non-Vegans Who Don't Understand

When the vegan tries to explain how difficult it is to be triggered to so many things involving animal use, they are often criticised as being:

1. Negative and no fun to be with,
2. Poor team players spoiling others' fun,
3. Pushy and telling non-vegans how to live,
4. Difficult and judgmental of others,
5. Over-sensitive and idealistic,
6. Unable to appreciate that change happens slowly,
7. Ridiculous for believing that animals hold equal value to humans,
8. Morally superior to non-vegans,
9. Uncaring about issues that don't involve animals,
10. "Greenies" who ought to go and get a "real job".

When Things That Held Promise Lose Value

The "Burden of Knowing" is so great for the vegan that things they previously found interesting and enjoyable often no longer satisfy. Planning holidays, moving to a new house, traditional celebrations, shopping, or career options often lose their shine and are considered trivial in relation to the emancipation of animals. Many vegans really only enjoy their free time with other vegans, knowing that together they are working to end animal suffering. Celebrations then become well earned rests from the task at hand.

Some vegans feel guilty for having any comfort or enjoyment, knowing animals have it so hard. I strongly encourage vegans to go beyond this and have "down-time," because the animals need us to be well-resourced and strong to speak on their behalf. Also, the vegan lifestyle is exponentially healthier, and the healthy, abundant, fun, and interesting vegan is a powerful advert for veganism.

The Anguish of Vystopia

The veil of deceit, lies, and ignorance has been removed from the vegan's eyes and they see the world through a very different lens. They have to live with the anguish of knowing that over 56 billion animals are being raped, tortured, tantalised, trivialised, stolen from, and murdered every year. They must also live with the ignorance of others who minimise, ridicule, resist, or ignore the reality the vegan tries to share. The vegan doesn't see economic progress but animal, environmental, and human suffering on a grand scale.

The vegan knows that animal abuse is directly related to human suffering in terms of environmental destruction, climate change, world starvation, ocean dead zones, Western illnesses, poverty, and greed. Their pain is amplified by a world that ignores the truth and relinquishes responsibility to powerful others, who dupe them into believing they have their best interests at heart. Like Edward

Snowden, discussed in the first chapter, who showed the world what personal privacy abuses happened behind closed doors, the vegan feels compelled to speak out and do everything to end animal suffering.

Many vegans acquire powerful resources to help them navigate their vystopia. Other vegans flounder, feeling like "strangers in a strange land" with no hope of ever finding home. All vegans however find it even more challenging to navigate the world of personal relationships with loved ones who are not vegan. We will discuss this in the next chapter.

Chapter 4

What Used to Work Doesn't
- Relationships With Non-Vegans

*Everything is expressed through relationship. Colour can exist
only through other colours, dimension through other dimensions,
position through other positions that oppose them. That is why I
regard relationship as the principal thing.*

– Piet Mondrian

Relationships can be a source of pleasure, growth and sense of
belonging. They can also be a source of conflict, unhappiness, and
distress. Psychologists, counsellors, and best friends know only too well
the amount of time spent discussing relationship problems. There is no
shortage of self-help books and programs on finding the perfect partner,
having a happy family, and why friendships succeed or fail. Why do so
many people have problems with their relationships? Let's look at this
generally before we look at relationships vegans have.

How Relationships are Formed

To answer the question about why people have problems with their
relationships, we need to look at why we form relationships in the first place
and how personal, social, and cultural myths influence our expectations.
Our family of origin is an example of a relationship we do not choose but
are, as the existential writer Heidegger says, "thrown into"[29]. We come
to know ourselves as a separate person only after others know us and

have shaped us through those interactions. Other relationships we choose, like friends and intimate partners. Some we interact with but decide on our level of interaction or exchange of more personal information, such as co-workers, colleagues or neighbours. Others we only interact with through more formal roles, like teachers, doctors, or police officers. Each of these interactions require a choice of different levels of interpersonal exchange and depth of intimacy.

How we interact is influenced by complicated dynamics, many of which are never made explicit and are based on myths or unquestioned assumptions. Our upbringing, time in history, culture, and own personality influence our beliefs and therefore our expectations and actions. As society changes, so does the backcloth against which our expectations exist. For example, in many cultures, respect for elders is an important collective belief. In Western society, this may have been a value up until the 1970s, but is now of less influence. Likewise, prior to the 1960s in Western society, it may have been unacceptable to have unmarried sex or cohabitation, or choose to be a single parent. However, this is now far more acceptable as a behaviour for people of all ages. Culture and religious belief affect these beliefs and expectations. Suffice to say, there are enormous differences in beliefs, values, and expectations between people despite collective influences coming from society and the era in which we are born.

We Are Doomed to Relate

From the moment we are born we enter relationships, not only with other people but with our surroundings. We come to know ourselves through relating to our physical and social environment, and develop a relationship with ourselves. As we form our own identity as an individual we relate to the world, its belief systems and different ideologies. We are always relating. Even in reading a book or watching a video on social media, we are relating to it and interpreting its meaning based on our own individual, social and cultural beliefs.

We bring this set of expectations and ways of interpreting the world to all our relationships with people. With a healthy enough background in trusting and communicating effectively with others, we can comfortably develop different levels of intimacy with people, work through differences and maintain healthy relationships. Often, we wonder why some people maintain the relationships they do, but it's always the case that we stay in relationships because they are meeting our needs. As circumstances change or needs no longer get met, new opportunities arise; some relationships continue and others end.

Values seem to be at the heart of whether relationships are satisfactory, maintained, or end. For example, even in relationships that don't meet important needs or in conflictual relationships, if there is an over-riding value that "staying together through thick and thin" is important, then people will tolerate unhappy relationships to stay true to that value of longevity and loyalty.

Veganism – the Deal-Breaker for Vegans?

Veganism is a value that is so powerful, it is very rarely relinquished even in the face of criticism, ridicule, lost intimacy with important others, or the ending of important relationships. I believe veganism as a value is so powerful because the vegan has emotionally connected with the suffering of animals. Their actions from that day on not only affect themselves, but are instrumental in adding to or ending animal suffering. There is little more painful to the vegan than being told they are selfish and only want others to be like them, when their value system is based on compassion, kindness, and lack of selfishness. They have seen the inherent and pervasive value shared by the majority of humans that we are superior as a species and that animals are there to meet our needs. Even if a person doesn't specifically voice this value, they collude with it through their consumer choices and inaction by maintaining their carnism.

Many vegans maintain relationships with significant non-vegans because they either rarely see them, or when they do time is limited. Family celebrations like Christmas or Thanksgiving are enormously challenging for vegans, faced with over-consumption of animals. They may have negotiated with their family to minimise animal use or cook vegan when they visit during the year, but the non-vegan family often consume meat for these traditional celebrations. However, because it is only for a short term, the vegan may find a way to navigate this. The same goes for long-term friendships when meetings are sporadic. However, in intimate relationships, immediate family you live with, or people you see every day at work, the challenges are greater.

The vegan has had their eyes opened and the world will never be the same again. They now have to relate to their family, friends, and partners armed with this overarching value within all the existing challenges of these specific relationships. No wonder they feel they are so alone. Not only do they have to live with the "burden of knowing" about the systematised cruelty against animals, they now feel responsible for sharing this knowledge, knowing that people they love are unwittingly colluding with it – until they too see the truth.

Challenges Facing Vegans in Relationships.

a) One to One Intimate Relationships

Many relationships exist where only one of the couple are vegan. When someone becomes vegan after learning about animal cruelty they not only want to tell everyone, they often believe that if they could only show their partner what is going on, they too will become vegan. When their partner refuses to listen or watch footage, is angry with their veganism, or insists on still stocking the fridge with animal products, the vegan's anguish is intensified as they face multiple challenges:

- Discovering the truth which has been hidden from them.
- Dealing with a partner who refuses to see or hear what is going on.
- Seeing their partner eat animals or bring animal products into the home.
- Being told not to "preach" to their family or force their children to be vegan.
- Being forced to choose to give up their veganism or end the relationship.

The vegan feels a huge sense of loss at many levels. Firstly, everything they believed to be true about the world feels like a lie. They then face either the ending of a relationship they were previously happy in, or staying in the relationship with a diminished emotional intimacy and understanding they once enjoyed. They become angry at what they have come to know, and when their partner refuses to discuss it, they can't understand how this otherwise kind, reasonable person could continue to collude with the horror of animal use. They live in a no man's land, deeply alienated, and wondering what went wrong when all they want is to live in a kinder world.

Veganism is provocative for many non-vegans who otherwise co-exist happily with their partners, despite very different interests or belief systems on things such as religion, career, hobbies, entertainment, or friends. I believe the reason for this is two-fold:

1. When a non-vegan discovers the truth, yet doesn't become vegan they either don't truly understand, refuse to believe what's happening, or do realise but refuse to change. That leaves their vegan partner desperate, knowing that if the person really understood, they couldn't continue to live as a non- vegan. As many clients say to me; "If someone really gets it yet doesn't become vegan, they must be a psychopath!"

2. Veganism requires a person to change their attitudes, mindset, actions and lifestyle. The biggest area of change involves what they eat, something they must do every day. People are often so steeped in their traditions, habits, and associations with the social or rewarding aspects of eating, they resist changing. They may also fear the resistance or criticism of others as well as the inconvenience. The vegan however sees such issues as trivial, and a small sacrifice to make to avoid hurting animals.

Here are typical things vegans say about the challenges they face in relationships with non-vegans:

- "My partner isn't vegan and I just can't accept it".
- "Everything would be perfect except my partner's not vegan".
- "I desperately want to be vegan and feel guilty and angry settling for vegetarianism".
- "Becoming vegan has thrown up lots of unresolved issues in my relationship, but veganism isn't something I will budge on".
- "It hurts me that my partner isn't vegan when not around me but I want to be with him and feel torn in all directions most of the time".
- "I feel lonely because my partner isn't as passionate as me about ending animal cruelty even though they now have a vegan diet".

- "I'm living a lie as I pretend to enjoy doing things with my partner, but can't wait to get back to doing activism with my vegan friends".
- "I didn't realise how dysfunctional my family is until I became vegan. They are totally unable to deal with anything emotional without going off the deep-end".
- "It's like sleeping with the enemy – I love my boyfriend but his body is a graveyard for dead animals".
- "Why am I told I'm superior when all I want is for my girlfriend to not be superior by spending her money on things that abuse animals?"

Client Example

Everything changed as Neville struggled to process what he'd learnt about the extent of global animal abuse. In a moment, the world as he knew it changed. He believed that by showing his partner of ten years what was happening, she would become vegan immediately. When she didn't, his world imploded a little bit more, and his anguish grew as he wondered whether he could live with someone choosing to contribute to the cruelty. They ate vegan at home and when out together, but he knew she didn't when not with him. She continued to buy clothes and makeup he knew caused extreme suffering to animals. She was shocked when he told her more detail but somehow managed to separate her desire to continue as she was and the industries who perpetrated such cruelty.

Neville is typical of many vegans I see whose partners don't immediately or eventually become vegan. They report feeling that they are "living with the enemy",

Client Example Continued

yet see their partner concerned about human rights or environmental issues. The gap between their own and their partner's compassion towards non-human animals causes a huge rift in the relationship, at a time when they seek more support to deal with the 'burden of knowing'.

Each vegan must decide whether and for how long they can live with a non-vegan partner. Some find the difference in values too great and others find a place where they can co-habit, believing one day the person will change, or accept they never will. For Neville, who chose to become an even more active animal rights campaigner, he sadly ended the relationship for his own and his partner's sake. He didn't want to judge someone he believed to be a good person, rather one whose bandwidth of compassion needed to be extended to encompass animals. He lives in the hope things will change, but knows that compromising his own values where animal cruelty is involved is not an option.

Why Won't My Partner Become Vegan?

People in relationships often want their partners to change aspects of their behaviour. For example, someone may wish their partner would lose weight, exercise more, drink less, or keep better company. There are big differences in what people tolerate in relationships and whilst they'd prefer them to change, it's often not a deal-breaker. After all, much of the desired change would actually benefit the other person. However, in the eyes of the vegan who is passionate about ending animal abuse, the benefit to their partner is secondary to the rights of animals.

The vegan is effectively asking their non-vegan partner to put aside any discomfort, ridicule, inconvenience, or resistance from others, because it's just wrong to be part of anything that exploits animals. This can be a hard sell to an otherwise perfectly reasonable human being, who is hearing about veganism for the first time. Not only do they have to deal with a partner who is often miserable because of what they now know, they are also being asked to tread the same path. Until the non-vegan emotionally connects with animal suffering, they are unlikely to change unless it's to hold on to their partner who says they will otherwise end the relationship. In many cases, a non-vegan partner, like other non-vegans, may emotionally abhor animal cruelty but other factors, including laziness, stand in the way of them changing. By learning about these and appreciating people's resistance, you can influence them to change rather than assuming they don't care.

Understanding a Person's Resistance to Change

- **Personality Differences**
  People have different ways of operating in the world including how they process new information and make decisions. Some people like more detailed facts and figures to form their views whereas others are more intuitive. Some are more logical when faced with new information whereas others base their decisions on values, regardless of logical arguments. By learning how different people typically operate, resistance can be reduced by presenting information differently.

- **Avoidance of Conflict**
  Many people fear conflict with other people and avoid talking about anything that will cause resistance, blame, or self-consciousness. They may lack the skills to have

conversations that matter or are overwhelmed by the emotions that accompany these conversations, saying things that others don't agree with or which affect other people.

- **Difficulty in Understanding One's Own Emotions**
  People have different levels of self-awareness and many find it hard to identify, label and communicate what they are feeling. A person who struggles with their own emotions may avoid doing anything that causes them any anxiety because they struggle with the self-consciousness that results.

- **Social Pressure to Conform**
  Enormous pressures exist to get people to conform to "normal" behaviour, and those who resist are often rejected from groups they value. Some people fear standing out, feeling self-conscious or lonely, although by conforming they often face internal conflict between their real values and their actions. As veganism becomes the norm, some individuals will change because that's the socially acceptable thing to do.

- **Limited Capacity for Empathy**
  People's ability to imagine the suffering of other living beings varies. Some feel deeply for their own family, yet struggle with feeling or expressing concern for strangers. Veganism requires emotional connection with a different species and is beyond many people, whose bandwidth of compassion must be expanded to include animals. This requires compassion towards these

people and finding ways to reach them, for example through a domestic animal they fiercely protect.

- **Apathy Regarding the Bigger Picture**
  People are not always willing or desire to be part of the solution for society's problems. The vegan who suffers from vystopia feels compelled to act to be part of the solution. Not everyone feels such responsibility for righting society's wrongs, and veganism is no exception. The non-vegan may see veganism as extreme, requiring them to commit their life to converting others.

- **Avoidance of Existential Angst**
  Learning about the extent and practice of industrialised cruelty towards animals is a shock to most people. They are forced to ask, "What else don't I know?" This causes enormous existential anxiety, and a deep sense of discomfort about the meaning and basis upon which someone's life is based. Becoming vegan dismantles the foundations of individual truth, and many people find this too distressing to face despite being against animal cruelty.

The vegan must face living with a partner who either refuses to discuss veganism, or vehemently resists and has their emotional defence mechanisms firmly in place. For some this is a painful reality they live with but for others, ending the relationship is the only way because the alternative is untenable.

b) Family Relationships

Living in a Trance

Our family influences us from the moment we are born and the ideals, values, and expectations we learn there continue to follow us throughout our lives. Existential philosophy explores the experience of what it is "to exist" in the physical, social, and ideological world. Existential writers talk about "trance-like» behaviour and social conformity, and how it limits us in how we live our lives. Heidegger talks about the "*They Self*"[30] and Nietzsche "*The Herd*"[31], both showing the power of society on how we experience ourselves and others and it all starts in the family. In "*The Myths of Life and the Choices We Have*" (Mann 2005)[32] I call it the *Group Myth*. The *Group Myth* is the unquestioned assumption that, "*It's better to be part of a group than be an individual*".

The *Group Myth* is so powerful that we can lose a real sense of who we and others are. The following quote by Cooper (1972:11)[33], although written in flowery existential language, sums this up:

> *"One of the first lessons one is taught in the course of one's family conditioning is that one is not enough to exist in the world on one's own. One is instructed in detail to disown one's self and to live agglutinatively so that one glues bits of other people onto oneself and then proceeds to ignore the difference between the otherness of one's self and the self-sameness of one's self. This is alienation in the sense of a passive submission to the invasion of others, originally the family other".*

Family Dynamics and Communicating Veganism

In conversations, body language, tone of voice, facial expression, and gestures all add meaning to the words we use. When we have a vested interest in a relationship, we tend to automatically interpret their body language based on assumptions of our shared history and past conversations.

Example

In conversations with family, you might regularly hear them say, "Here we go again!" when raising a topic and you raise your eyebrows. For example, when you talk about a subject of conflict with a sibling and you raise your eyebrows during the conversation because you're unclear about something they said, it's likely that they'll unconsciously react to your subtle facial changes and automatically say, "Here we go again!" In a fraction of a second, their attention moves to your shared history rather than what you're saying. A button has been pressed and the conversation becomes emotionally charged. You might unconsciously realise this and do something to get them to focus on what you're saying. Automatically, you adjust the tone, content, or urgency of your message. This then triggers a reaction in them which you pick up, making you feel judged, criticised or laughed at, and the whole interpersonal dance continues. The person you've been speaking with shifts their attention away from the emotional content of the vegan message to the emotional energy in your interaction. The result is that the listener shifts their attention to how they feel about *you* rather than how they feel about animal cruelty. This is why so many vegans say it's their family that's the hardest to talk to about veganism.

71

When vegans are talking to acquaintances or the public, they don't have the history, known dynamics, and power issues they have in their families. In face to face exchanges within the family, they face an interpersonal complexity which is key to understanding the depth of the vegan's trauma. In conversations about animal cruelty, we want our family to connect emotionally with the effect of their food choices. Often though, their emotional reactions are outside of the confronting material itself and more focused on the dynamics within our relationship with them.

Client Example

Many young vegans who have not yet left home or school become powerful leaders, and influence their whole families to become vegan. Others struggle every day, seeing conflict develop between some family members who subsequently choose this path and others who don't. Family meal times where animals are served are excruciating events for most vegans, but unlike older vegans, the young person living at home feels there is no way to avoid this except always eating alone.

Alison faced an even bigger challenge as her father bragged about his kangaroo and pig hunting and brought home fish he had killed. She started to hate her father, believing him to be some sort of monster, devoid of any feeling who enjoyed abusing animals. She became more alienated and started cutting herself and limiting her food, all symptoms of someone feeling trapped and desperately out of control. She was diagnosed as anorexic when she came to see me.

After several sessions with me, Alison learnt to understand her feelings of anger, grief, and loss, and re-frame what was happening to her.

She began to see her father as someone more fearful of losing his friends and community status than someone seeking pleasure from the cruelty his sports entailed.

She learnt powerful ways to understand her emotions and improve her communication. She talked to him about his emotional connection to the family dogs and cats, and used non-judgemental ways to get him to consider other animals whose lives equally matter to them. She discovered that people have enormous defence mechanisms that stop them emotionally engaging with animal cruelty. But there's often a way through and by re-directing the anger and powerlessness she felt from herself and non-vegans, she became more influential in getting him and others to change.

The Enemy Within –
Living As the Only Vegan in a Non-Vegan Family

Here are typical things vegans say about the challenges of living within a non-vegan family:

- "My partner is almost vegan but I feel sick as she cooks meat when her children visit".
- "My partner says I'm being over-sensitive when the nanny breaks agreed rules and feeds our child meat or dairy".
- "The family continually make fun of my eating choices at the table".
- "I feel undermined when my family ridicule my choices saying it's just a fad".
- "My family force me to eat animals and tell me when I'm an adult I can choose for myself".

- "I feel guilty when my mum defends me to my dad and it causes big arguments".
- "I just can't reconcile that my family are decent people yet know about animal cruelty and refuse to change their habits".
- "How can my partner get other social injustices like child poverty but not empathise with an animal being tortured"?

Not all family conversations about veganism are so troublesome. Often one or more family members do become vegan after hearing about what happens to animals, the environment, or the improved health benefits of a plant-based diet. The best thing a vegan can do is to be a great example of a happy, adjusted, open-minded, caring person who also happens to be vegan. Then they are one step nearer to becoming vegan with a diminished ability to shoot you, the messenger, for being so difficult.

c) Family of Origin and Extended Family Relationships

We've seen how existential ideas can help explain the influences of family in our identity, beliefs and behaviour. When new families are formed through partnership, differences become apparent. Conflict is often monitored when people aren't living under the same roof, although parental influence on adult children can cause divisions between intimate partners. Here are some typical things vegans say about these influences:

- "My in-laws don't usually interfere but became really angry when I refused to serve milk products at my child's christening".
- "Christmas with the meat-eating in-laws was the most painful experience of my life and I'm a cancer survivor!"

- "My siblings use my veganism against me to score points with our parents"
- "I always knew dad bullied mum and she doesn't speak up for herself but it upsets me when she says she's vegan yet eats meat with him to keep the peace".
- "My in-laws say I have no right to impose my values on my children and make them vegan. It's not only vegans who bring their values to the dinner table".

Why Do Families Resist Members Becoming Vegan?

The late Albert Schweitzer said, "The problem with man today is that he doesn't think" and that human beings tend to copy other people, conforming to what they believe is acceptable or "the right thing". Presumably he also meant women. Such conformity inside or outside of the family is not entirely a conscious choice, but rather an unconscious acceptance that one's culture, societal norms, or the "way things have always been" are correct.

Sanctions for not adhering to certain norms may result in being excluded from the family or community. For example, a family may reject an individual who decides to marry outside their faith or culture. Other families may not agree with their children's choices, but do not reject them. Instead they may appeal to the individual to change, encouraging them to embrace their own culture by behaving in a collectively acceptable way.

Understanding Resistance

Not all families respond the same way to a family member becoming vegan. Personal ridicule or criticism can be levelled at the person, with complaints about how difficult they make things for everyone else, or how family celebrations will never be the same again.

Remarks often relate to the family's disappointment that the vegan is "difficult", and upsetting the way the family operates. Often complaints focus on personal disappointment and appeals to lost intimacy and shared traditions, rather than appealing to wider cultural norms.

Why is resistance personally focused when a family member becomes vegan, and generically focused when a family member changes faith, or marries outside their culture? For example, a family who adhere to strict Judaism would most likely resist a member of their family marrying a Muslim. Likewise, a European couple in a strict Christian denomination might be resisted in their attempts to adopt a child from a family of a different nationality whose country broadly does not uphold Christianity. In each case, an appeal might be made to their actions being against their culture.

I believe it's because the family's non-veganism is personally affronted by the vegan's values, in ways that other actions or beliefs may not be.

Example:

Imagine a family with strong beliefs about who their daughter should marry in terms of race, religion, or sexual orientation. One of the daughters announces that she wishes to marry outside these boundaries. If tradition is valued and her parents believe it is more correct for people to act in prescribed ways, they are likely to exert pressure on her to conform to what they believe is acceptable. They may criticise, ridicule, implore, or even eject her from the family until she changes her ways. The daughter may or may not stick to her choices while she is attacked for not respecting theirs. However, while the daughter may seek parental approval for her choice, she is unlikely to expect her brothers and sisters to copy her.

76

This is what makes the choice to be an ethical vegan different. The person who chooses to be vegan wishes for their family and the whole world to be vegan. Individuals who choose to be vegan not only want their family to accept their choices, but they want them to become vegan too.

The Difficulty of Speaking to Family about Veganism.

Vegans typically report the following about talking to their non-vegan family:

- They advise their family why they have become vegan and the trauma and anger they feel in relation to the extent of animal abuse in society.
- The family may be open-minded and discuss the vegan's choice more fully. Alternatively, they may criticise the choice because of its negative effect on family habits and traditions.
- Having told their family of the extent of animal cruelty, how their daily choices involve using products and services that abuse animals, vegans expect the family to make the same vegan choice. They say things like, "If my family really understood my pain and were compassionate people, they would be vegan. How could they not be?" This of course is the same challenge a vegan faces with a non-vegan partner.

This is why the vegan suffers enormous angst in living in a non-vegan family. Conversations are more difficult because they take place within cultural and family norms that provide a shared sense of identity. I believe the vegan's angst is existential in nature, and increases the angst of everyone involved.

77

d)   **Relationships with Friends**

One of the symptoms of vystopia is loss and grief for how the world used to be. Vegans often report desperately trying to hold on to their existing friends but claim that things "just don't feel the same". There is a loss of intimacy, with conversations or activities seeming trivial now the vegan knows the truth. Often friendships are kept with non-vegans at the expense of not speaking up. It seems to be rare for friendships to flourish when the non-vegan refuses to talk about veganism or bars the vegan mentioning it after the initial explanation.

Relationships of long-standing seem to be more able to withstand the changes because each friend enjoys the connection based on their journey together through life. However, if too much time is spent with these long-these term friends, cracks start to appear as differences become apparent which push them apart. This causes a deep sense of loss for the vegan who is often told, "You are not as much fun these days" and they want to scream out, "It's not about me! It's about you continuing to abuse animals!"

Here are typical things vegans say about relationships with non-vegan friends:

- "I was furious when my friends said, why don't you worry more about people? They are suffering too you know!"
- "I became full of rage when my friend bought a pashmina scarf in-front of me and tried to hide it. That means they knew they were doing something wrong but were too selfish not to do it!"
- "Why am I always the one to compromise my values and go to non-vegan restaurants, just because I'm the odd one out?"
- "Everything that doesn't involve ending animal suffering is trivial and sheer entertainment to me these days".

- "Are people so blind they don't get upset at the cruelty involved in things like rodeos, circuses, horse-racing, fox-hunting?"

Such realisations become defining moments for vegans who know something has been lost that can never be recovered. It's as if they have come out of the "Garden of Eden"; their innocence is lost and they are forever a stranger in a strange land. They feel lonely, misunderstood, and are criticised and labelled misanthropists. As one vegan said, "I would kill myself were it not for knowing I would be abandoning all these animals who rely on my voice".

Navigating Relationships With Non-Vegans

Relationships with non-vegans, as we have seen, can be enormously challenging. The 'burden of knowing' is an onerous one, compelling us to play our part in ending animal suffering. Some vegans seem to navigate relationships with their non-vegan families, partners and friends, yet feel a deep sense of anxiety witnessing their collusion with systems that maintain the status quo. Others maintain distant relationships with family and end previously happy intimate relationships with significant others who do not become vegan. Either way, the cost is great, revealing the strength of the vegan's commitment to being part of creating a world where animals, planet, and people are not abused.

Chapter 5

The Illusion of Freedom in an Unfree World

The evidence shows us that the story we have been given is a lie, one that brave researchers have been exposing for some time. The best way for us to deal with that reality is to recognise it and not to give it power over ourselves. We don't have to be taken in by the illusions because, if we seek transformation, we need truth as our constant companion".

– Richard Dolan

Every positive move forward in human history is because people come together and speak out saying, "We can do better than this and we will". Our history books reveal ample examples of physical slavery of human beings which today seem barbaric and totally unacceptable. We are horrified by accounts of abuses towards Roman slaves, the African slave trade, and the Civil Rights Movement of Black Americans. We find it unacceptable that entire sub-groups are disenfranchised and unable to vote for nothing more inconsequential than the colour of their skins or position in society. We also realise that there was a time when such human rights abuses were accepted by powerful sectors of society – that was until people spoke out against such prejudice by privileged groups.

We are the first to sign petitions or support causes to free people from long and treacherous work in sweat shops, or being abused by profiteers who pay little to no wages, who keep them trapped in cycles of despair and economic slavery. For example, workers trapped in retail sweat shops, blood or conflict diamonds, or cocoa bean farming.

The Depth of the Deception in the Non-Vegan World

As vegans, our eyes have been opened to the mass injustice towards animals and we're left wondering how we didn't know know about it before. We see the extent of systematised cruelty and wonder what else we need to question. Upon becoming vegan there is a seismic shift in how you see the world, and you shift from trusting what you have been told to questioning everything you've ever heard.

Veganism opens a door to the realisation the non-vegan world that is truly dystopian in nature. You now see everything through a different lens of lies and deception and for these questioning few, vystopia is taken to a new level. Living in this dystopia is exacerbated as you face the collusion of those who still hold the view that everything they've been told, on the whole, is true. The vystopian's sense of alienation is acute and you feel unable to find a way to open people's eyes, and instead you're labelled as opinionated or a conspiracy theorist.

Whilst it's not possible to build a comprehensive list of all the world's lies, we can identify where mass deceptions are being perpetrated to broadly hide abuses towards people, the planet or animals. This chapter provides vegans with analogies of other abuses and deceptions to act as an invitation to others to question the extent of the lies they too have been told.

By providing examples to discuss the extent of mass deception, we have a tool to explain our vystopia and show non-vegans how more informed choices can change the outcomes for our world – beginning with our everyday consumer choices.

In Chapter 6 we look specifically at how to engage people in these conversations. These communication tools, used with the following analogies, will help you as a vegan be more influential when talking about veganism.

Modern Day Slavery

In 2013, a report in the UK newspaper the "Daily Mail" revealed that workers were paid £1.12/hour to produce iPhones and iPads for Apple Inc[34]. Many of the workers performed monotonous and tedious tasks for ten hours at a time, and in one factory in the Chinese town of Shenzhen, eighteen employees had killed themselves. The factory managers asked for suicide nets to be erected after nine workers killed themselves in the space of three months.

Blood diamonds[35], also called conflict diamonds, is a term used where people are held at gunpoint to mine diamonds in war zones. The diamonds are sold to finance warlord activity.

In 2013, it was estimated that 1.4 million children aged between five and eleven worked in agriculture in cocoa growing areas[36]. Approximately, 800,000 of them were engaged in hazardous work. Whilst indications are that these numbers have reduced, companies that transform these into high end luxury chocolate for the Western world continue the abuse.

All of these examples of physical or economic slavery constitute nothing more than modern day chain-gangs. Physical slavery continues, but tends to be hidden from the world, and when discovered, is abhorrent to most people. We expect progressive countries to condemn nations who fail to protect their citizens and don't afford the same rights to people of different coloured skin, gender, nationality or creed. However, whilst profit remains the main motive of unscrupulous corporations, people will continue to be trapped in economic slavery and hidden from view.

Are We Still In Chains?

What if we have never really escaped slavery? According to The Global Slavery Index, there are more slaves now than ever in recorded modern history. In 2016, it was estimated that there were 45.8 million people in some form of modern slavery in 167 countries[37].

Also, in countries where we believe ourselves to be free, what if we are even more incarcerated than ever before through mental chains? History holds ample accounts of how people are persecuted for their beliefs when they run contrary to the norm or privileged few. For example, the Spanish Inquisition, Medieval Witch Hunts, religious persecution, Prohibition, and political views contrary to a powerful elite.

These examples of silencing those who speak out against the norm ensnare the wider population to avoid speaking out against a very limited diet of choices. Today we are told we have a lot of choice in how to live our lives and that we have a say regarding the physical, social and ideological world we live in. We are told we have democracy and that our vote counts and yet we have to choose, often between the lesser of two evils. Often, we can't even discern between the different political parties, and many become disillusioned and don't even vote. This leaves the door open for some less ethical politicians to take advantage of the apathy and forge ahead with their own agendas, with scant concern for the interest of people, the environment, or animals. The interested reader is directed to writers like Noam Chomsky, John Pilger, and Seymour Hersh, who examine how the powerful few benefit from continuing physical and mental slavery, much of which we can't even identify.

Even When We Are Told We Are Free

People in the West are told they are free within a market economy to exercise choice and quality of life. However when we look closely, the majority of human beings appear to have created lifestyles for themselves that are simply not sustainable. In the book

"Communicate: How to Say What Needs to be Said, When it Needs to be Said, in the Way it Needs to be Said" (Mann 2012)[38], I refer to the interviews I personally held with fifty-four senior executives about their jobs. Without exception, their stories revealed that their private lives, as well as their public lives in the organisations they served, were reminiscent of animals in factory farms. Their collective silence masked their suffering, and they had helped to create their own small pens in which they were unable to turn around, and were denied a chance to exercise their curiosity, creativity, and freedom. Like non-human animals bred for industrial use, they are part of an industry that de-individualises them and requires them to contribute to economic success, often at the expense of everything else. Sadly, this is typical for both executives and other workers of large, modern organisations that focus on profit at the expense of people, the environment, and animals.

How Deep Is The Rabbit Hole?

When movements develop to change socially entrenched ways of thinking, they face enormous resistance from the majority. Veganism, the philosophy of non-speciesism, is no exception. Changing beliefs take place within a social and cultural context, and mental slavery where we rarely question why things exist as they are. This stops us even imagining a world that is different. It's not just veganism that faces resistance. For example, living in a money-free world, the existence of aliens, free energy, natural healing, and miracles are often dismissed outright because we are enslaved in a mental gaol. We stop being curious and the most dangerous comment arises: "We have always done it like this".

1. Politics

Whilst most people in the West don't face every-day fear of their own governments, freedom is far from the democracy people are told they enjoy. Many believe the government is there for the people and that they, the people, have democratic rights. This is questioned when considering the extent of corporate funding and lobbyists in politics. Most countries have sold off their infrastructure such as power plants and power lines to large multi-national companies that pay no tax. As these infrastructures were paid for by the tax-payer, one would like to believe the tax-payer has a say in what happens to these assets, and are compensated if they are sold. We all know this is not the case.

We are told that the government is there to protect and serve the people. However, the Patriotic Act[39], passed ostensibly to fight terrorism, was actually more about targeting US citizens at home in mass surveillance programs. Why does the government need to look at every email and phone call in the name of national security, while funded by the taxpayer?

In terms of animals, governments attempt to criminalise people exposing abuses towards animals in industrial farming, under the guise of Biosecurity (AgGag) laws. The USA is not the only place that appears to have draconian laws. People who speak out against such abuses often come up against a system that exists to stop them. The Australian Federal Government is pushing for changes to the Espionage Act, so a journalist merely receiving classified material faces fifteen years imprisonment[40]. Likewise, Australian law makers are attempting to change the electoral regulations to force civil action groups such as GetUp or Greenpeace to be affiliated with a political party and thus subject to political finance laws. This effectively ties up these organisations in red tape leaving little funds to operate.

2. Economics

Media and government in the West talk about the economy as if it was a specific entity, beyond the control of individuals. Regardless of what economic system exists where you live, it's assumed it offers the means by which you can partake and benefit from the production of goods and services. It's accepted as an even playing field where, with education and effort you can benefit, whilst the government exercises control to protect the most vulnerable of society. Yet unemployment, homelessness, and people living below the poverty line, paints a very different picture.

An even playing field couldn't be farther from the truth. Huge conglomerates become powerful influences controlled by very few people with deep pockets, and become impenetrable. Systems theorists at the Swiss Federal Institute of Technology in Zurich took a database listing of 37 million companies and investors worldwide and analysed all 43,060 trans-national corporations and share ownerships linking them. They built a model of who owns what and what their revenues were, and produced a map of economic power and corporate control. They discovered that global corporate control comprises a dominant core of 147 firms which are intertwined, and together control 40% of the wealth in the network. A total of 737 control 80% of it all[41].

Within this system, animals become mere economic units referred to as stock rather than sentient creatures. As long as animals are seen as stock units and property, they will remain enslaved by the economic system.

3. Science and Innovation

We live at a time when anything that can't be proven by scientific rigour is not taken seriously, yet science as we know it is only a couple of hundred years old. When things are discovered like gravity or the electromagnetic spectrum, it doesn't mean they didn't exist before, we just didn't ask the right questions or have the tools to discover them. We don't have to understand how the sun generates energy, but we can still enjoy its warmth, just as the radio frequencies used by mobile phones existed before we knew how to use them.

Imagine you lived in the 1950s and someone said, "Imagine having a hand-held device, the size of a packet of cigarettes, that you can use to see and talk to someone on the other side of the planet?" They would have laughed at you and labelled you as crazy - just as Marconi, who invented the radio, was taken by his friends to an asylum for saying he heard voices. So what ideas or innovations do we now laugh at, saying it's not possible, yet in fifty years times will be commonly accepted as normal? For example, anti-gravity technology, free energy, or teleportation.

The innovator is always pushing against the closed-mindedness of what is known as the prevailing Zeitgeist or Spirit of the Time. The vegan offers a paradigm shift in how and what we think is possible. Despite the irrefutable evidence that veganism is a healthier, fairer, kinder, and more economical way to live with a smaller footprint, many will refuse to entertain it until a sizeable proportion of the population say it's normal.

4. Medicine

The World Health Organisation in 2008 estimated that 65% of global deaths are due to lifestyle diseases such as tobacco, poor diet, and alcohol[42]. This figure was as high as 80% in low and middle-income countries. Despite this estimation, allopathic medicine continues to seek cures for these ills whilst ignoring key factors. Films such as "*What the Health*", "*Forks over Knives*", and "*Plant Pure Nation*" reveal that most modern illnesses can be reversed with a whole-food, plant-based diet. So why aren't medical professionals listening to their peers who challenge the status quo of what contributes to health and illness? The answer can probably be found in entrenched beliefs and, in many cases, the source of funding and sponsorship. For example, in Australia, 2006, the chief scientific body in Australia, the CSIRO, published the second edition of its massively successful "*Total Wellbeing Diet*". The diet encouraged high meat consumption, despite its own scientists pointing out that a meat-heavy diet was related to colorectal cancer. It appears that the research the CSIRO based its book on was funded by the Meat and Livestock Industry; a body set to benefit from increased meat consumption.[43]

Alternative medicine is ridiculed as quackery because it's seen to lack scientific rigour. As mentioned before, empirical scientific research is considered god-like and the arbiter of all truth. Any positive outcomes of naturopathy, homeopathy and acupuncture for example are laughed at by allopathic practitioners as "all in the mind". However how is it that sugar pills, commonly known as placeboes, commonly out-perform pharmaceutical drugs? Benedetti's research in the mid 1990s mapped out many of the biochemical reactions responsible for the placebo effect[44]. He uncovered a broad range of self-healing responses that not only relieve pain but elevate mood, sharpen cognitive ability, alleviate digestive disorders, relieve insomnia, and limit the secretion of stress-related hormones like insulin and cortisol. Why is it then that any challenge to allopathic medicine is quickly dismissed?

One factor that might indicate why alternative medicine is dismissed relates to the multi-billion-dollar industry behind the medical profession.

In the USA alone, the industry was worth $446 Billion in 2016[45]. Entrenched beliefs about medicine that serve a rich few keep people firmly in the trance.

5. Education and Employment

In the West, people are told they must get an education in order to enter the job market. They have to decide early on what subjects to take at school or college to enter certain careers. This focuses them on becoming specialists, usually to ensure they can earn money and support themselves. However, this doesn't prepare them for the uncertainty that inevitably exists in an ever-changing world. According to Professor Boehn (2017), professor of computer science, "Eighty percent of jobs that will exist in 2025 don't exist today; we have to prepare our students and graduates for a world that's essentially not possible to prepare them for".[46] However, the existing education system seems unable to adapt quickly enough to move from training specialists to life-long learners, able to generalise their skills to solve a variety of problems.

Looking for a job in today's economy is done in a competitive environment, reminding us that we are part of the economic machinery. We assume we have to get a job to make money, in order to live and increase our choices. People seek numerous ways to become financially free, believing that if they can achieve this, only then will they be free to choose how to live their lives. In our existing economic system, few ever achieve this and the rest are exhausted from the economic treadmill with no room to stand back and question their own lives, let alone the world they live in. We are told "This is how it is". The western lifestyle dream, frequently called the American Dream is just that – a dream which is unattainable.

Because our education systems don't teach us to creatively think and solve problems, when new ways of thinking about how we can work and live are presented, they are quickly dismissed as unrealistic.

Forward thinkers like Michael Tellinger (2013)[47] offer fresh ways to re-think our education, society and our individual contributions. His vision of a world based on Contributionism, one that doesn't require money yet isn't socialism or communism but based on people doing what they love, requires us to come out of the trance and entertain a utopia. In this system, people, environment and animals wouldn't be economically abused through the pursuit of profit with no responsibility. However, as Einstein said, "We need a different level of thinking to solve the problems that created them".

6. Religion

As human beings we struggle when unable to make sense of things we don't understand. For example, questions like, "Why are we here?" "Why do so many people suffer?" leave us feeling anxious and afraid. There is no shortage of people or ideologies that rush to fill the void stating, "This is the Truth". Religions or philosophical beliefs talk about after-lives and whether we believe in heaven or hell, karma, reincarnation, or meaninglessness, we all find it difficult to live with un-knowing. There are many religions that claim to have a monopoly on the truth, and each of us must decide where we stand in relation to what they offer. Many religions result in us relinquishing responsibility for our own lives, instead blaming our challenges on being "born in sin" or "brought into the world to suffer". These are just belief systems and the net effect of them is to stop questioning.

Religions as belief systems are huge causes of separation and division on the planet, often used as the excuse for invasion, ethnic cleansing, and preferred ways of living. At its extreme it results in bloodshed as evidenced by the Great Crusades and major wars, and at its least renders individuals powerless and able to only choose from a small diet of choices of how to live and be in the world.

The vegan is often blamed for being like a religious zealot. However, instead of assuaging their existential anxiety by imposing an ideology on others, the ethical vegan is a voice speaking out for the oppressed non-human animal. The vegan invites us to refuse to be part of one of the biggest forms of superiority on the planet; speciesism. By becoming vegan, we not only stop financing animal cruelty through our consumer choices but positively impact our environment, health and potential to create a more compassionate world.

7. Environment

There are numerous examples where something billed as either having good or little to no negative impact on the environment, later turns out to have disastrous effects on the environment, people, and animals living nearby. For example, nuclear power is touted as a clean, safe energy source but disasters like Three Mile Island, Chernobyl and Fukushima reveal this is not so. Disasters on these scales are hard to hide, particularly as people rapidly become sick or die from radiation poisoning. This is not the case with environmental abuses which occur steadily, beyond the public eye and where cause and effect are not clear. For example, fracking, the injection of chemicals into the ground to dissolve rock so oil and gas can easily be extracted, has major detrimental effects on groundwater supplies. Many people have never heard of "chemtrails", the alleged weather modification practices of spraying aerosols in the atmosphere. Those who speak out against them are quickly labelled as conspiracy theorists. However, in 1976, the convention on the Prohibition of Military or Any Other Hostile Use of Environmental Modification Techniques[48] was held, making us question why such a convention would be necessary if weather modification technology didn't exist.

Most people have seen campaigns imploring us to restrict our domestic water use such as taking shorter showers, investing in water-efficient appliances, and limiting the watering of our gardens. The implication is that restricting our water use will have a major effect on dwindling water supplies. In Australia, over 67% of water is used for agriculture whereas only 9% is for household use (CSIRO)[49]. Water use through food consumption is 90% of a household's water use (Rutherfurd, Tsang & Tan (2007))[50]. This implies that for any water-saving effort to have an effect it should be concentrated on indirect water use. The United Nations Environment Programme (UNEP) (Hertwich 2010)[51] concludes that: "A substantial reduction of climate impacts from agriculture would only be possible with a substantial worldwide diet change, away from animal products".

The vegan knows that we have been lied to about the effects of carnism and that not only is non-veganism a travesty against animals, it's destroying our environment, and making people sick in the process.

8. Speciesism

Speciesism is the belief system that says that some species are more valuable than others or that different members of the same species have different value. For example, in Western culture companion animals are given legal protection against deliberate acts of cruelty, whereas animals raised for food do not share these rights. Fox (2017)[52] says, "The term 'speciesism' was coined by psychologist Richard Ryder in 1970 and refers to a prejudice similar to sexism or racism in that the treatment of individuals is determined by their membership of a particular group. Just as less value is placed on certain people based on their sex, gender, race, sexual orientation, or other defining characteristic, so too are animals afforded even less consideration and moral worth based on the fact they are a species other than human".

When vegans talk about animal rights, they face resistance from non-vegans who say that human beings have greater value than animals and that animal testing for example, is justified if it reduces human suffering. Even many feminists, outraged by real or perceived inequalities or sexualisation of women, still eat animal products directly sourced from hijacking of animal female reproductive systems.

These trance-like beliefs and actions of humans believing they are superior to animals, and entitled to eat, use, and wear animals, is deeply distressing to vegans who seek equality for all sentient beings.

Client Example

David, like many vegans, developed a deep disgust for human beings after discovering animal factory farming. His tolerance for non-vegans was very low and if they didn't immediately or very soon become vegan after he told them, he relegated them to people who were despicable. This led him to become very depressed and hopeless about the potential of creating a vegan world. At the same time, he felt that his time away from animal rights campaigning was wasted, making him dread going to work. He lost interest in any activities he felt were relaxing or pleasurable and he stopped going to the movies or exercising. He was reaching burnout when he came to see me.

Anger is a normal part of the grieving process. The grief of suddenly seeing the truth that's hidden from us is often channelled into a dislike for anyone who is seen to be part of the deception. By working through this anger and realising other people have been similarly duped into being part of the cover-up,

David developed more compassion towards others. He realised that people are so shocked that such deception is possible, they resist this new information in order to prevent their world collapsing.

Escaping Your Own Rabbit Hole

We live our lives and make decisions within these socially prevailing influences (hidden and explicit) in an economic environment that leaves us scant time to even think or research these things. We are socially programmed to believe that this is normal and to fit in, you too must be normal. It's hard to break out of our own trance and engage with this process. We are also in our own personal rabbit holes and conditioned to think, behave, and feel in a certain way, so we don't know we need to ask questions.

How does the average individual even begin to look at their own mental boundaries and ask different questions of how they are refusing to see anything differently? Veganism is a rising tide of social awareness, questioning the mental gaol that has speciesism at its root. Linked to this are the social and ideological institutions that cement the mental enslavement and the resultant collusion with prevailing norms. We have examined ten of them above.

The vegan has a challenging task ahead. After all, they are lifting the veil on beliefs, values, and behaviours the majority of the population are engaged in. When someone suggests a different viewpoint, it causes anxiety as people are challenged to see the world as not fixed and objective, and they must ask; "What else don't I know?" The vegan has become aware of the systematised cruelty towards animals and the trance-like collusion with this dystopian world. They are suffering from vystopia and now must navigate this new land and open other people up to the possibility that there is a better way to treat animals, people, and the planet with whom we share our lives.

Veganism – The Ultimate Medium in Trance-Breaking

The vegan's beliefs and behaviour challenge the social norms the majority of people live by. Becoming vegan requires an individual to change their thinking and actions in ways that affect them everyday. Each day, the vegan makes choices to seek out products and services that don't directly or indirectly abuse animals, and this takes time and energy. For the ethical vegan, this is not a problem but for someone not distressed by animal use, it can be seen as an inconvenience and of little importance.

The vegan has also learnt to question other societal beliefs many take for granted. The above list, whilst not exhaustive, indicates numerous areas which indicate that finding the truth is not always so easy. In our time-poor world, people are either too tired, indifferent, or confused to question the norm. The vegan is a modern-day whistle-blower who not only implores us to change but questions everything, and for many, this is so painful and a deep existential crisis which many are ill equipped to navigate.

Resource:

This chapter identifies numerous ways in which social and cultural norms influence behaviour. In "*The Myths of Life and the Choices We Have*" (2005), I identify eight myths or unquestioned assumptions that are personally, socially, or culturally determined and which limit the extent of our choices and decision making. It attempts to break us out of our own individual trances and ask different questions about who we are and the infinite possibilities we have in how we want to live our lives.

A full explanation of these myths is outside the remit of this book but you can access a free copy of this book via http://claremann.com to find out how these myths influence your own life and how you can begin to break through the chains that limit your thinking of what is possible.

Chapter 6

Creating a World to Belong To

Cowardice asks the question: Is it safe?
Expediency asks the question: Is it politic?
Vanity asks the question: Is it popular?
But, conscience asks the question: Is it right?
And there comes a time one must take a position that is neither
safe, nor politic, nor popular -- but one must take it simply
because it is right.

– Martin Luther King, Jr.

The world for the vystopian, as previous chapters reveal, is challenging and confronting. The burden of knowing is so great for so many that without help, a vegan world where animals are protected and treated with respect, is a distant dream. Others see the growth of veganism and are optimistic and channel their energies into making this happen. For every vegan, a times comes when they either "break down" or "break through". How can the vegan break through and be part of the solution? How can we create that Vegan Utopia where animals, people, and planet are living in peace? How can you move from survival to waking up each day, excited to be part of this eagerly anticipated better world?

Client Example

Rachel spent several years in a deep depression after learning about the live animal export trade, which resulted in her becoming vegan. She was horrified by how animals suffer arduous trips overseas, but it took her some time to realise the deep shame she carried, since she had been born into a family overseas that was involved in the live trade. As a child, she hadn't realised what her family's business entailed as they ensured she didn't see what happened to animals in abattoirs and religious festivals. Upon learning about live export, she started to put the pieces together and realised that her family's wealth had been built on the backs of animal suffering. Whilst it had not been her choice, she felt tainted with the actions of her family, yet couldn't face confronting them or jeopardising what was already a difficult relationship. Instead of expressing her anger and confusion, she internalised her pain and became severely depressed.

As a psychologist I have never seen someone depressed without the presence of anger directed inwards, rather than being worked through constructively. Depression can be a form of "learned helplessness" (Seligman 1992)[61] where the person feels powerless to change their situation and feels that anything they do won't change it either. Despite Rachel exploring the shame she felt about her family background and the pain of knowing about animal suffering, she couldn't move out of her depression. However, when she decided to use her specific skills to speak out for animals, her depression started to lift. She learnt that meaningful work and making a difference is a powerful way to transmute one's pain into a life worth living.

The Good News

As indicated in an earlier chapter, there continues to be a major increase in the uptake of veganism around the world. New vegan options are appearing in supermarkets, with entire sections created for vegan food. A huge number of vegan documentaries continue to be released, many being distributed on NetFlix and watched by millions of the mainstream. Each day the media mention something about veganism, from celebrities adopting plant-based diets to those speaking out against cruelty. We are truly witnessing a rising tide of awareness with veganism as the biggest social justice movement of our time. Despite the existence of the dystopian world, there is a lot to be optimistic about.

Being the Invitation

To play our part in creating a vegan world, you must become the best invitation you can be to others. In order to do that you must put your own oxygen mask on first and work through the grief and anguish of what you know, so you can become resourced to be the best voice for the animals. Although understandable, you have to move through the depths of anguish and misanthropy to envision a vegan world. As you will see later in this chapter, this not only makes your life enjoyable but is essential to influence change at a global level.

Here are 10 things you can do to resource yourself for the journey:

1) Practice Good Nutrition

To remain healthy, vibrant and energised, it's important to adopt a wholefood, plant-based diet. It not only contains the essential range of nutrients for optimum health but also facilitates healing and cell repair in the body, slows down the ageing process, and alkalises and energises the body. Many vegans play scant attention to nutrition other than to ensure no animals are harmed for their meal. Avoid the highly processed vegan diet which not only inhibits optimum health but results in sugar cravings, irritability, or moodiness, and feeds the state of vystopia.

2) Exercise Regularly

Find a regular exercise that you enjoy and which provides you with solitude or an opportunity to meet with others. Not only is exercise essential to build strength, stamina and flexibility, it's directly linked with mood. Depression can be lifted with regular exercise as it's associated with the release of endorphins in the brain. Exercise helps you sleep better, aids digestion, and raises energy levels.

3) Relax and Have Fun

Many animal advocates want to spend every spare bit of time they have in reducing the suffering of animals. Only then is their vystopia assuaged and they can live with the burden of knowing. Others feel guilty that they once financed animal cruelty with their consumer choices and won't allow themselves any enjoyment or ease. Remember the animals need you next week, next month, and in the coming years to advocate for their freedom. If you burn out you won't be able to help them, so factor some relaxation and fun in your life with like-minded others, so you can resource yourself to go much farther in the vegan movement.

4) Develop a Positive Mindset

Your thoughts, feelings, and experiences are intimately linked. When you feel something negative, the stress hormones adrenalin and cortisol are released and you feel negative sensations in your body. You're likely to then say something like, "I feel awful, angry, or disgusted". This triggers more thoughts which release more stress hormones and this interaction results in labelling the emotion where you say, "I am angry or defeated" (or another label). Over time, the connection between your thoughts and feelings becomes so intertwined and automatic that the body remembers and it becomes a habit. The slightest trigger or association with the initially provocative information automatically results in a negative feeling and labelling of yourself as angry, resentful, depressed, or other similar words. When you see, hear, or think of something related to this topic, before you know it, you feel all the emotions as if you were experiencing the original provocative event.

The same thing happens with positive emotions. This time, happy hormones are released. Dopamine, serotonin, and oxytocin help you feel hope, safety, and trust. In short, whatever you spend your time thinking and feeling creates your personal reality, and to change this, you must change the thoughts, feelings, and actions. By deliberately focusing on positive things you start the process of change, but where negative thoughts are too deeply embedded, meditation can assist.

5) Meditation

Your mind and body do not know the difference between real and imagined events. For example, when you wake up in the middle of the night after a nightmare, your body shows all the symptoms of fear as if there were a real threat such as: increased heart rate, anxiety, fear, and sweating. Once you realise it is only a dream, you change your mind and personal reality. Yet moments before, you felt that the threat was real.

To create a new *Personal Reality of Thriving as a Vegan*, you must spend time focusing on the world you wish to create in your thoughts, feelings, and actions. I encourage you for as little as five minutes each day to visualise and experience the positive vegan world you want to create, as if it was in the present moment. These steps are a powerful way to set a clear intention and associate it with an elevated state of positive emotion. Research from neuroscience and quantum physics reveals that our imagination doesn't just create a feel-good factor, it is correlated with physical reality. In short, what you concentrate on, you create.

The more you focus on the positive effects of veganism rather than the stress and anxiety of consumerism, environmental damage, animal cruelty, or the fear-mongering media, the more positive you will become. You then become part of the rising tide of social awareness of veganism and bring that day closer. People around you will notice the difference and are more likely to trust you, because there is congruence between what you say and what you truly feel. You will avoid coming from a place of judging others so they are more likely to listen because they feel you have their best interests at heart.

Visit the following link: http://veganpsychologist.com/ meditation to download a 15 min meditation "Visualising a Vegan World".

6) Minimise Stress

Stress is your reaction to life's external events as well as internal memories of experiences. It's your body and mind's way of telling you things are out of balance. Make a list of what causes you stress in your life and see what you can take out to create more ease. Avoid spending time around negative people or overcommitting to things that put too much pressure on you. Learn to say no and set boundaries with other people. Adopt stress-reducing practices like yoga or relaxation techniques so you can regularly bring yourself back to a state of calm, especially after advocating.

7) Educate Yourself

Commit to life-long learning about veganism so you become a well-informed individual who is able to speak with conviction and impact. Having facts and figures to hand will provide you with a level of gravitas to any discussion with non-vegans, who are often quick to attack and ask you for evidence. Over time you will acquire more information and by practising having conversations about veganism, you will eagerly look forward to people asking you questions, knowing that you can back up your arguments with lots of relevant and powerful information.

8) Gather Support

Across all losses and stressors in life, the biggest factor in a person working through difficulties is the extent to which they have social support. Having others with whom you can share your feelings and seek guidance goes a long way in helping us recover and make sense of life's challenges. Invest in your relationships, knowing that people need your support too. Many vegans only feel totally accepted by fellow vystopians, particularly when their pain is linked to what they know about animal exploitation. However, vegans also have lots of other concerns. Give and receive support, but ensure you jointly develop ways to navigate through the pain rather than allowing negativity and misanthropy to result.

9) Become Your Best Ally

Many vegans traumatised by vystopia have low self-esteem and blame themselves for not doing enough to help animals or convert other people into vegans. This self-blame can result in destructive habits and self-punishment, rather than being your own best friend. Become your best ally and through mindfulness, meditation, exercise, and other self-care regimes, you will develop a sanctuary within yourself which will sustain you over the years. You will also become an example of a calm, confident, and decent person who people aspire to follow.

10) Become an Exquisite Communicator

Communicating veganism can be challenging, because people think you are directly criticising their lifestyle and choices and they resist that more than the reality of where their food, clothes, cosmetics, and other consumer goods come from. Thus, you must learn tools and techniques that enable you to have difficult conversations easily. Here are some key skills to help you:

- Challenge your own assumptions about other people's intentions.
- Remain open minded and don't assume non-vegans don't care about what you are saying. Resistance is

often due to self-consciousness or feeling blamed for the world's problems, rather than resisting the content of your message.

- Develop active listening skills and ask more questions, check out what other people mean and adjust your message when they don't understand.
- Pinpoint the "hooks" or topics that interest them and use these as a way to engage their interest. Common hooks include the environment, wildlife, animal ethics, or health.
- Focus on moving people along a Continuum of Awareness (see below) from having no interest in veganism to becoming vegan. Speak to people where they are at, realising that most of us require repeated exposure to new ideas before we change our own beliefs. You don't have to do all the work. Realise that they will also hear about these issues from other people, TV, adverts, and social media, and make a connection with subjects they are interested in. Ensure that your input to their continuum of increasing awareness is the best you can offer.

By putting in place ways to resource yourself, you can then move from depression to optimism and start to engage, educate and influence people to become vegan. Remember, when someone becomes vegan, they too enter vystopia and need help to work through their anguish and be part of the solution too. Many people see a distressed vegan and resist because they don't want to feel like that. You become attractive when you become the best example of a vegan who has not only worked through vystopia but is a much happier, healthier person with a purpose.

Become an exquisite communicator so you influence people to change. Learn to have difficult conversations where emotions are very high and people have different opinions and views. As a passionate vegan, you may want to tell them everything you know about the issues, but this can result in resistance. It's not always what the other person is interested in hearing, and forcing your own agenda won't establish rapport or allow you to explore other subjects later. Bombarding someone with details of animal cruelty in factory farms, while relevant and important to share, may result in resistance if they have indicated they are most interested in health or environmental protection. When you have explored their interests, you can add more information to expand their understanding.

It's important to realise that you don't have to convert everyone on the spot and, a useful concept to understand this is *The Continuum of Awareness*.

The Continuum of Awareness

1. resistance   10. ready to change

Imagine that every person you meet (including yourself) is on a journey towards increased consciousness, compassion, and awareness. Let's imagine it runs from 1 to 10, with 1 representing absolutely no interest in veganism, and 10 indicating a person wanting to hear more and likely to become vegan soon. Your job is to listen carefully to assess where they are on the continuum and provide information, insights, and education to move them towards increased awareness.

You do this by identifying what is known as "hooks"; topics that literally hook the person in by providing them with something about veganism they are concerned with. For example:

- Health
- Environment
- Animal Cruelty
- Job Security
- Spirituality
- Economics
- Traditions
- Social Norms
- Philosophy
- Freedom of Thought

For example, someone might ask you, "Where do you get your protein?" If you answered, "It's not all about you - do you know how animals suffer in factory farms?" you will make them confused or angry, because they are asking you something about health. Remember they may have never heard of a factory farm and certainly don't know as much as the passionate animal activist. By responding to their question about health, you establish rapport and can move into providing information about other issues including animal social justice.

By using hooks, you provide people with information to expand their thinking on an issue. If you use information that doesn't relate to their interests or current world view, you'll lose rapport and they'll resist you. You don't have to turn someone into a vegan right away. Some people see images or hear information and become vegan right away; others take time. Your job is to move them along the continuum so they emotionally engage with the information and come to the conclusion on their own. After all, you don't want someone to have a knee-jerk reaction to an image and say they have changed their mind, yet later revert to their old habits. You want them to change permanently. Time spent nudging them along the continuum provides greater probability that any changed attitudes, values, or behaviour will be permanent.

The Story of Gigi Pizzeria

A woman I didn't recognise, said to me, "You know it all started with you?" She reminded me that as her customer in a health food shop in Sydney, Australia, she was curious as to why I returned a product containing milk. I had explained what happens in the dairy industry, and how calves are taken from their mothers so humans can consume their milk. She was shocked, and I returned the next day with literature from Animals Australia so she could read more about it. I left believing I had done my best and didn't hear from her until I saw her three years later.

She explained that she was horrified by what I told her and decided to do her own research. Over several months, she explored what happens to animals in the industrial process and her worst fears were realised. Not only was my account true, but her eyes were opened to the billions of animals who suffer each year for our food, fashion, cosmetics and entertainment.

Although she made changes to her own life, the weight of knowing about animal suffering meant she had to go further. She called her family together to share what she had learnt, a brave thing to do because her son ran a well-known and successful Italian restaurant.

Through her advocacy, her family made the collective decision to no longer collude with the suffering of animals for the sake of tradition, profit, or tastebuds. They also decided to turn their successful restaurant vegan. That restaurant was Gigi Pizzeria in Newtown, an inner-city suburb of Sydney.

This example reminds us to communicate without judgement. Sometimes we never get to hear the effects of our advocacy and other times we hear those wonderful words, "I've become vegan!" I had the rare opportunity to learn how my advocacy contributed to this extraordinary family putting ethics before tradition and profit, and choosing to "veganise" their restaurant. However, most of the time, we don't get to hear what happens.

Learn to Collaborate

It's important to surround yourself with people who understand, share your values, and are positive. Apart from feeling supported and understood, larger principles underpin such social encounters that influence the growth of veganism. By learning about these you will be encouraged to collaborate with others for reasons other than finding your own tribe and overcoming the alienation and loneliness that vystopians suffer. We'll now explore three important factors to take into account of how social change happens.

The Tipping Point

Marketers are aware that the uptake of products and services appears to follow a certain pattern. For example, in the 1990s, few people believed that the mobile phone market would explode to such a point. People who saw the market's potential and invested early on are known as innovators, quickly followed by the early adopters[53]. Uptake then gradually increased and suddenly appeared to gather momentum. Uptake starts to reach a critical mass as the early majority come on board, quickly followed by the late majority, these two groups making up the bulk of the market.

Others either follow or give in, for example, the grandmother who realises the only way to contact her grandchild is to get a mobile phone.

This is also the same for changes in collective beliefs and ideas in society. For example, the early protagonists for the Abolition of Slavery were the innovators and early adopters. They faced enormous resistance by those who benefited from the trade. As this movement gathered momentum, it reached what Gladwell (2000) calls the "Tipping Point"[54]: "The moment of critical mass, the threshold, the boiling point", and a phenomenon that describes the pattern associated with mysterious sociological changes. Gladwell says, "Ideas, products, messages and behaviours spread like viruses do"[55].

Increasingly, teenage vegans are referred to me who say, "I just had this awareness and know it is wrong to eat animals". Many of them hadn't seen anything on veganism or spoken to anyone about animal exploitation. It is my belief that this is an example of what Jung (1969) calls the "Collective Unconscious"[56]; the structures of the unconscious mind which are shared among beings of the same species. This is encouraging for vegans who often feel helpless and can't see how a vegan world will happen in their lifetimes. Concepts of the Tipping Point, Collective Unconscious, and Entrainment are indications of how and why veganism appears to be growing rapidly.

Entrainment

In 1665 Christian Huygens[57], whilst working on the design of the pendulum clock, found that when he placed two of them on a wall near each other and swung the pendulums at different rates, they eventually ended up swinging in at the same rate[58]. This is due to their mutual influence on one another. He called this Entrainment and defined it as the tendency for two oscillating bodies to lock into phase so that they vibrate in harmony or synchronise over two or more rhythmic cycles. This phenomenon of matter synchronising appears to be universal, appearing in chemistry, pharmacology, biology, medicine, psychology, sociology, astronomy, and architecture. For example, women living in the same household or sharing the same workplace find that their menstrual cycles coincide and often the heart muscles of people in close proximity begin pulsating in synchronicity.

Vegans often feel depressed, wondering how sufficient people are going to change for veganism to be the new norm. They tell me that they despair for people they believe are so selfish they will never stop eating or using animals. The concept of entrainment is an encouraging one for vegans, reminding us of the importance of playing our part in being the example we want others to "entrain" to. By shifting our focus from how awful the world is to taking action every day to mirror the vegan world we seek, we are creating a new norm to which others will entrain. Other sections in this chapter provide practical ways in which we can collaborate better with other vegans to speed this process up.

Spiral Dynamics

The original book on "Spiral Dynamics"[59] is a complex read, revealing the hidden codes that shape human nature, create global diversities, and drive evolutionary change. The authors talk about the magnetic forces that attract and repel individuals, form the webs that connect people within organisations, and influence the rise and fall of nations and cultures. The book tracks our historic emergence from clans to tribes to networks and inter-connected networks. It identifies seven variations on how change occurs in individuals, society and leadership.

I believe the relevance for veganism is in appreciating there are different levels of consciousness in society. For example, a vegan passionate about the ethical treatment of animals would be faced with resistance from a hunter with a more tribal level of consciousness (according to Spiral Dynamics model). It would be like two people from different planets communicating. Another example would be a community outraged by the influence of veganism on local employment, as demand for dairy reduces. By understanding where other people or groups are coming from, we can adapt the way in which we communicate. If we talk ethics and non-speciesism to people focused primarily on job security and local or cultural traditions, we will face resistance. In this chapter, I talk about using the "hooks" to engage people with their concerns, and then introduce other topics nearer to the ethical imperative of veganism.

Client Example

Angela was an active animal advocate and regularly attended rallies and vigils and signed petitions. She felt pleased to be part of animal groups she believed were making a difference to the lives of animals. However, the more involved she got, the more frustrated she became with people who took a more welfare-based approach to animal social justice rather than an abolitionist one. She became angry at people who campaigned for better conditions for animals, or encouraged things like Meat-Free Monday or a gradual transition to a vegan diet. Instead of expressing her views constructively, she started to attack anyone who didn't take an abolitionist perspective and many people left online groups as a result of the animosity she fuelled in online discussions. Angela's reaction is typical of many vegans who empathise deeply with animal suffering and believe progress is only possible when animals are not used in any way by humans.

Not only was Angela deeply distressed by seeing the suffering of animals first-hand, she was further immobilised by her anger and frustration, and wondered if change for animals would ever be possible. By channelling her anger away from criticising the shortcomings of others, she felt more empowered and less exhausted. Whilst holding strict abolitionist views, she started to see that criticising others was counterproductive to helping animals as whilst people were fighting amongst themselves, they were not focusing on animals. She learnt to be more compassionate for where people are in their journey, and researched how social change comes about. Whilst she would prefer that people change immediately, she realised that people often don't change that quickly and the net outcome – a better life for all animals – was a better focus than differences in ideologies.

Finding a Community

To maximise your advocacy, join a community who are collaboratively working together towards a common goal. The best communities are those who share a very clear vision of the compassionate and kind world they wish to create rather than engaging in in-fighting and politics. These unfortunate actions occur when people haven't sufficiently worked through their vystopia and fuel their grief and anger in dysfunctional ways. Groups that help members work through their difficulties, improve their communication skills, and understand group dynamics are those who truly collaborate towards collectively aligned objectives, underpinned by the global goal of veganism.

Principles of Collaboration

Many organisations comprise people working in silos on different projects, who only engage with other groups when absolutely necessary. Members tend to identify primarily with their own group and often resist collaborating and learning from others. To improve the situation, a consultant would work to remove barriers, increase communication between and within groups, and create mutual understanding to achieve better collective outcomes.

One of the biggest limitations to improved working is related to the unquestioned assumptions people hold about what is happening. Without high levels of self-awareness, people often fail to question their assumptions about other people and how things should be done. These preconceived ideas result in prejudice and stereotypes that inhibit people connecting and collaborating for mutual benefit. It's important to teach people ways to continually question their assumptions and own their part in creating the outcomes of every interpersonal interaction they have. This, together with learning to communicate effectively and skillfully navigate differences, has the potential to create relationships, groups, and organisations that achieve superior outcomes and are satisfying communities to work in.

Vegan and Animal Advocacy groups are no different from other groups or larger organisations. They comprise diverse types of people with different backgrounds, viewpoints, skills, and ideas of how to get the job done. High levels of emotion associated with animal welfare and veganism provides one of the biggest opportunities and yet one of the biggest challenges. High emotions may compound misunderstandings and differences of opinion and result in conflict, whilst strong emotion, when channeled effectively, is a uniting motivator for action.

The Collaborative Vegan Community

How can high levels of emotion and commitment to veganism be channeled constructively to enhance animal social justice rather than create conflict, despair, and frustration? For example, we often see high emotion and criticism expressed in social media, which is damaging if there is no ability to effectively work through the resultant conflict. Technology provides amazing tools to connect and collaborate but we must still learn the skills of managing ourselves effectively and creating good relationships with exquisite communication in environments of high stress.

By applying the wisdom of lessons learnt from psychology to animal advocacy groups and focusing on four main human areas, we can take full advantage of the benefits offered by technology:

- Individual self-awareness
- Group dynamics
- Communication skills
- Organisational culture

Individual Self-Awareness

In order to contribute your best as an employee or volunteer in animal social justice, one of the best things you can do is to develop high levels of self-awareness. You must become aware of when your buttons are pressed, of the patterns we repeat in relationships, and how we come across to other people. By identifying your unquestioned assumptions, you can avoid hasty judgements, challenge your conclusions, and remain open-minded. This increases your ability to form good relationships with other people and collaborate effectively.

Group Dynamics

A group comprises individuals who identify with the group and share a common purpose. The extent to which group norms are adhered to determines how cohesive the group is. Groups often avoid talking about difficult subjects, fearing it will cause conflict. Whilst counter-intuitive, it is essential for groups to "air their differences" and create a platform of trust and mutual respect in which opinions can be discussed. Without this, groups never become truly effective, because unresolved differences inhibit effective collaboration.

Communication Skills

You must learn to effectively communicate with other people by creating rapport and having meaningful conversations with people, many of whom will resist or criticise the message of animal social justice or veganism. There are skills you can learn to confidently convey difficult information effectively without aggression or backing down, even when the information is distressing. With help and practice it does become easier.

Organisational Culture

An organisational or group culture comprises an explicit and implicit understanding amongst members of how things operate. An effective culture fosters the collective needs of people who identify with it and unify under a cohesive set of rules. This occurs with effective leadership, a shared vision, and people feeling they belong and know the rules within which the organisation operates. Without a culture that fosters commitment, contribution, and mutual respect, politics, in-fighting, and sabotage often occur.

We are living in a time in history when we have the means to communicate instantly with people all over the globe. People can be called together, physically or virtually, within hours rather than the months it previously took to galvanise people into action. In order to truly benefit from these wonderful new communication platforms, we have to ensure we invest in our individual, group, and cultural development. Only then can we effectively collaborate and come together with other groups and be an even greater collective voice for animals.

By increasing our self-awareness, understanding group dynamics, and applying exquisite skills of communication, we have an opportunity to partake in dramatically changing the fate of billions of animals who currently are subject to use and exploitation by humans. The sheer number of animals whose lives stand to change for the better makes this the largest social justice movement on the planet.

Whatever animal or vegan group we belong to, we are effectively doing the same work. Each of us is attracted to different aspects of animal social justice. Some of us work on the frontline, involved in direct or uncover work like factory farming or vivisection. Others work on lobbying governments and industry to make changes in legislation and policy. Some of us enjoy working locally with hands-on wildlife care, whilst others simply make more ethical consumer choices about the products we purchase. All these actions contribute to a kinder world for animals and ultimately, for people and the planet.

It starts with us as individuals. How we choose to conduct ourselves is an act of leadership and an example to others of how we want the world to be. We must each be the best we can be, a self-reflective individual who can proudly answer "Yes!" to the question "Would I follow me?"

Becoming Part of the Global Vegan Relay Team

Imagine you are a part of an international sales team who have been tasked with the job of selling the most amazing solution for vast majority of the world's problems? You hold the solution for the current global challenges to human health, environment, social justice, the economy, consciousness, and spiritual growth. The customer is every person on the planet. What training will your team need to convey the solution and match it to the problems the customer is facing? Surely a team tasked to deliver such promises, would have a clear strategy and sales process. Or would they wing conversations with customers and get annoyed at them when they don't buy the solution offered?

Well, if you are a vegan reading this, you are part of this sales team. You may feel resistant to selling, believing that the current financial and economic system is based on selling and perpetuates a system of greed, and are averse to selling products and services on the back of human, animal, and environmental suffering. If so, how do you feel that you've been recruited to this new vegan global sales team? Also, if we use this sales analogy, there are other customers who'll benefit from your endeavours – the animals. And they are silent, you're unsure they even know you're working at a global level to improve their quality of life and you can't easily canvass their feedback on how well we're all doing our job.

How Do You Feel About Selling Veganism?

Faced with this responsibility, you may feel you're facing this task with no real training, only skills you've acquired along the way. You may feel alone in the process, or wish you had more information to hand to convince people to buy the solution of veganism. You may long for linguistic mastery to deal with buyer resistance or would like help in up-selling them from vegetarianism to veganism – the crème de la crème solution which involves their biggest investment and yet the greatest reward.

You won't have the chance to meet all the sales team, practice selling with them, or ensure your sales materials are well branded and professional. However, we're all relying on each other to do a great job of offering the solution. It's hard because no-one likes rejection and when we offer the solution, our customers often deny they have a problem, claim the solution doesn't work, prefer existing solutions, or can't afford it.

The best thing you can do is adopt key principles from sales psychology and understand that sometimes the sales cycle is short and sometimes long – some people buy on the spot, others buy lesser priced products and when satisfied make higher investments. There'll be customers who say "no" or "not yet", because they're insufficiently convinced of the solution. Sometimes we have to wait because it's not until sufficient people change that they decide to keep up with the Joneses or become convinced by the latest celebrity.

What Do You Need To Be a Great Vegan Salesperson?

1. Mind-shift change

You must believe in your ability to communicate and sell veganism. If you feel anxious and tongue-tied, your whole neurology will work against you. When you're discussing animal cruelty, for example, you'll often feel anxious and in pain. When this discomfort or anger occurs, blood flows from your frontal cortex to the "reptilian brain" at the back of your head. This is the "fight or flight" red zone where it's difficult to stay calm, confident and convincing[60]. The same thing occurs for the listener, resulting in resistance and comments like, "Don't tell me any more!" The good news is that there's a contagion effect and if you can keep calm and empathise with the person struggling to receive this challenging information, you'll influence their blood to flow to the frontal cortex with the increased likelihood that they'll listen to you. You must regularly practice techniques to remain calm like meditation, positive self-talk, increasing confidence through communication mastery, and seeking out social support from other vegans.

A useful technique to calm yourself and move the blood to the frontal cortex in readiness for these challenging conversations is Emotional Freedom Technique (EFT). For a short video on this technique, visit http://claremann.com/endstress

Understanding neuroscience and the parts of the brain responsible for decision making and emotional responses is invaluable, because common knowledge amongst sales people indicates that people buy with emotion and back up their decisions with logic. The information you share must evoke a sufficiently emotional response requiring them to want a solution, which can be reinforced with logic. Such logic is influenced by providing them with facts, figures, and evidence that veganism works. People buy from people they like so by learning to be empathic, non-judgemental, and supportive of where they are in their journey, they'll learn to trust you (and other members of the vegan sales team) and say that magic phrase every vegan wants to hear: "That's interesting; tell me more."

2. A Sales Process

When engaging people to talk about veganism, it's best not to wing your conversations or play them by ear. Whilst you don't want to be too prescriptive, it's important to develop a sales process, to move them along the continuum from "not interested" to "tell me more" or, even better, "I am becoming a vegan!" Note, you may need several conversations for them to become vegan and they may not all be with you. They'll also be influenced by videos,

TV adverts, media reports on animal cruelty and other sources of information. Once you start the conversation, they won't be able to see issues around animal cruelty and veganism in the same light. New information about the subject will activate what you've told them so it's important that you make a good impression and provide information to back up your claims. Here are some key principles:

a) **Make a contract**.

Tell the person what you'd like to talk to them about and get agreement to discuss it. When they say yes, you can refer back to this later when they say, "I can't continue discussing this". Their comment isn't then a signal to stop, but merely to modify the intensity of the information you share.

b) **Use questions to elicit their motivation**.

Ask lots of questions to ascertain their understanding, interests and problems around health, social justice, environment and social concerns. Then you can position the vegan message so it meets their needs. If you insist on talking about animal cruelty when they're asking about diet or environmental sustainability, they'll switch off. Listen, ask questions, and provide information relative to the person's need. You can add other information later when they say, "Tell me more".

c) **Handle resistance**

It is normal and predicable for someone to resist changing their attitudes and behaviour. When a person resists what you're telling them, instead of sighing and judging them as blind and selfish, see resistance as positive. Appreciate that you've elicited an emotional response in them, they're uncomfortable and will want to remove that discomfort. They can choose to ignore what you've told them (which is often more difficult than they think) or seek a solution.

Resistance in any sales process occurs for four main reasons and in the context of veganism, typical responses include:

i) Money: "I can't afford to be a vegan and buy fresh fruit and vegetables".

ii) Time: "I don't have time to prepare vegan food".

iii) Need: "I'm not sufficiently convinced I could live without meat or dairy".

iv) Urgency: "I'll think about it later as it's not pressing for me now".

v) Trust: "I don't believe you".

By seeing resistance as positive, indicating that you must answer their concerns, you'll become empowered rather than believing it's futile and some people will never change.

d) **Sales materials to support your arguments**

Provide information and evidence that veganism is the solution. Use testimonials and case studies of people who have benefited from adopting veganism. Send links to videos or articles with evidence of the positive changes that result when they adopt veganism.

e)   **Provide the solution**

Provide as much information as you can relevant to their interests, questions, and willingness to receive it. Follow up with information to back your claims and always make a time to talk to them when they have had time to review it.

Remember, you may not close the sale and hear them say 'Yes, I'm becoming vegan'. You are part of the global vegan sales team and your contribution is to influence people every day to adopt veganism. Likewise, when someone tells you they're becoming vegan, it is likely that another member of the team influenced their decision.

3. Exquisite communication skills

As indicated throughout this book, you must become a great communicator so you can influence people to become vegan. Partner with non-vegans and talk to them as someone who has also been duped by society and industry to live in a non-vegan world. Learn to listen and position your responses relative to their needs, gain rapport, and build a relationship based on trust so they don't shoot the messenger when they receive challenging information.

Communicating veganism is like running a relay race. You tell somebody something, later they see a TV advert or something on social media and one day, the tipping point comes, their resistance reduces and they choose veganism or as I prefer to say, "They return to their vegan birthright". Some may never become vegan in their lifetime but every conversation we all have contributes to a vegan world becoming the norm. Your job is to be a great salesperson so you don't let the team or the animals down.

What Next?

In a gentle way, you can shake the world.

- Mahatma Gandhi

It's time to transform the anguish of your vystopia into effective action for change. Your anguish must become a powerful intrinsic motivator, burning within you, only assuaged by you taking inspired action every day. Those actions must be aligned with that bigger vision of the compassionate world you want to be part of.

Not everyone needs to be on the world stage or doing frontline work with animals. We all have different gifts which, when shared regularly, have the capacity to change the world. Find out what your gift is in this global movement, refine and practice it regularly. It may be something you love to do but don't allow yourself because you think it takes attention away from advocacy.

For example, if you love movies and cooking, invite people to your home for an exquisite vegan meal, followed by a vegan film and conversation. If you love bush-walking, take your friends walking and casually raise the effects of consumer action on the environment and wildlife – and don't forget to include vegan treats. Someone I know rents out his holiday house with no television but a video recorder and library of vegan documentaries. Such actions, when practised regularly, move people along their individual continuums of awareness and collectively move us all towards the tipping point of global change.

Resource yourself every day to share the truth and break other people out of their trances. Learn to communicate calmly, factually, and powerfully so they start to question what they've been told and become uncomfortable colluding with the deception. Most people are nearer to veganism than you think because they recognise the truth when they hear it.

Remember, when you drop a pebble into the water, you don't know where the ripples stop. One day, you return a product because it contains dairy and a restaurant becomes vegan. I wonder how many others have become vegan because that restaurant led the way, each inching us towards our Vegan Utopia.

I look forward to seeing you on the journey!

Resources

Watch

Cowspiracy (environment)

Dominion (Australian animal rights)

Earthlings (vegan/animal rights)

Economics of Happiness (economics)

Food Inc (factory farming)

Food Matters (food/health)

Forks Over Knives (veganism/health)

Hungry for Change (food/health/ethics of food)

Norm (social conformity)

Peaceable Kingdom (vegan/animals rights)

The Corporation (economics)

What the Health (health)

Read

Becoming Vegan Express Edition (2013) Brenda Davis & Vesanto Melina

So Why Become Vegan (2011) Sandra Kimler

Staying Positive in a F*cked Up World (2018) Ash Nayate

The China Study (2016) T. Colin Campbell

The Ethics of What We Eat (2006) Jim Mason & Peter Singer

The Minimalist Vegan: A Simple Manifesto On Why To Live With Less Stuff And More Compassion (2017) Masa Ofei & Michael Ofei

Ubuntu Contributionism (2013) Michael Tellinger

Why We Love Dogs, Eat Pigs and Wear Cows (2011) Melanie Joy

Psychological Support

You know how crippling it is to live in a non-vegan world? CLARE MANN is a vegan psychologist who understands those challenges.

Programs and resources to:
- turn despair into positive action
- have conversations with ease
- communicate with impact
- influence others to change
- thrive and enjoy life as a vegan.

 VeganPsychologist.com

VEGAN VOICES

training and resources to

thrive as a vegan

app available on Apple and Android

www.vegan-voices.com

Glossary of Terms

269
: A bull who was rescued as a calf by anonymous activists, days before his planned slaughter.

Abolitionism
: Referring to the freedom of black slaves in early 19th Century America

Animal welfare
: An animal's physical and emotional needs.

Biosecurity
: Preventative measures designed to protect a population from biological harm, such as infection.

Bobby calves
: Newborn male calves, routinely removed from their mothers within 24 hours of birth. Slaughtered within their first week of life, or within three months of life if raised for veal meat.

Burden of knowing
: The burden or pain of emotion and responsibility which comes with certain knowledge.

Carnism
: A term coined by vegan activist and psychologist Melanie Joy. Relating to the classification of certain animals as edible food, and the acceptance of routine animal harm as "normal" or "necessary".

Chem trails
: A trail left in the sky by aircraft, believed by some people to contain chemical agents.

CIA
: Central Intelligence Agency of the United States of America.

Conspiracy theory	A belief that a particular organisation is responsible for an otherwise unexplainable event. Often linked to government or powerful organisations.
CSIRO	Commonwealth Scientific and Industrial Research Organisation; an agency of the Australian Federal Government.
Dystopia	A place or state, usually imagined, where everything is bad. Often connected with environmental degradation, widespread disease, or political totalitarianism.
Eating disorder	A psychological condition manifesting as disturbed behaviours surrounding food and eating. Examples include anorexia nervosa and bulimia.
Existentialism	A theory of philosophy focussed on the existence of an individual within the world. The theory holds that humans have free will, freedom, and the choice to define their own path in life.
Factory farming	A form of modern animal agriculture, with a focus on profit and efficacy over animal welfare.
Free range	Allowing farmed animals to roam outside of confined spaces. The definition of free range varies, and some small, confined spaces are still considered "free range".

Garden of Eden	A biblical reference to a beautiful garden containing the Tree of Life. Described in Genesis, the Garden of Eden is where God intended humanity to live in peace and innocence.
Mental anguish	A type of mental suffering which includes a variety of symptoms such as distress, anxiety, grief, or depression.
Misanthropy	A hatred, dislike, distrust, or contempt of humankind.
NSA	National Security Agency of the United States of America. Functions as the intelligence agency for the Department of Defense.
Self harm	Deliberate injury to one's own body, often connected with psychological disorders.
Speciesism	The belief that humans are superior to animals, and therefore animals may be exploited for human gain.
Stall free	The farming of pigs without the use of space-confining, movement-restricting stalls.
Systematised cruelty	The torture, cruelty, and exploitation of animals as part of a social and agricultural system, which is perceived as normal and necessary.
United Nations	An international government agency committed to world-wide peace, security, social progress, and human rights.

Uptopia	A fictional community or world in which living standards are perfect for each citizen.
Wilful ignorance	Keeping oneself in a state of deliberate ignorance, so as to avoid the responsibility and liability of knowing the facts.
World Health Organisation	An agency of the United Nations which specialises in international public health.

References

1   https://www.edwardsnowden.com/

2   https://www.asbestos.com/asbestos/

3   MOWAT. A.,CORRIGAN, J. and LONG, D. (2009) The Success Zone. 5 Powerful Steps to Growing Yourself and Leading Others. Australia:Global Publishing Group

4   https://www.aph.gov.au/Parliamentary_Business/Bills_Legislation/Bills_Search_Results/Result?bld=s1099

5   https://www.vegansociety.com/whats-new/news/find-out-how-many-vegans-are-great-britain

6   https://www.livekindly.co/vegan-statistics/

7   http://www.animalsaustralia.org/issues/dairy.php

8   https://www.creativespirits.info/aboriginalculture/politics/a-guide-to-australias-stolen-generations

9   http://www.animalsaustralia.org/features/nepal-ends-worlds-largest-animal-sacrifice-event-gadhimai.php

10   http://www.animalsaustralia.org/features/victory-bali-dog-meat-ends.php

11   https://www.carnism.org/

12   http://animalsaustralia.org/issues/codes-of-cruelty.php

13   https://www.forksoverknives.com/animal-agriculture-hunger-and-how-to-feed-a-growing-global-population-part-one-of-two/#gs.wq4ps30

14   https://news.un.org/en/story/2006/11/201222-rearing-cattle-produces-more-greenhouse-gases-driving-cars-un-report-warns

15   http://animalsaustralia.org/factsheets/animal_experimentation.php#types_of_research

I16   http://www.animalsaustralia.org/issues/

17   https://en.wikipedia.org/wiki/Dystopia

18   https://en.wikipedia.org/wiki/Misanthropy

19   http://www.269life.com/

20   http://whatthehealthfilm.com

21   RUSSELL, G. (2009) CSIRO Perfidy: The truth about CSIRO's bestselling, "scientifically proven" diet, and its cancer causing central ingredient. Australia:Vivid Publishing

22   https://www.youtube.com/watch?v=dvca71uSc3U

23   https://veganpsychologist.com/survey

24   https://www.youtube.com/watch?v=7i15OPuFvmA

25   http://www.banliveexport.com/

26   http://www.animalsaustralia.org/issues/kangaroo_shooting.php

27   http://www.animalsaustralia.org/features/puppy-factory-problem.php

28   http://www.animalsaustralia.org/issues/introduced_animals.php

29   HEIDEGGER, M. (2008) Being and Time. USA: Harper Perennial Modern Classics; Reprint edition

30   ibid. see 29.

31   NIETZSCHE, F. (2009) On the Genealogy of Morals. UK: Oxford University Press;

32   MANN, C.E. (2005) The Myths of Life and the Choices We Have. Australia: Koromiko Publishing.

33   COOPER, D. (1972) The Death of the Family. 2nd Edn. UK: Pelican

34   http://www.dailymail.co.uk/news/article-2103798/Revealed-Inside-Apples-Chinese-sweatshop-factory-workers-paid-just-1-12-hour.html

35   https://en.wikipedia.org/wiki/Blood_diamond

36   https://en.wikipedia.org/wiki/Child_labor_in_cocoa_production

37   https://www.globalslaveryindex.org/findings/

38   MANN, C.E. (2012) Communicate: How to Say What Needs to be Said, When it Needs to be Said, in the Way it Needs to be Said. Australia:Communicate31 Pty Ltd

39   https://en.wikipedia.org/wiki/Patriot_Act

40   https://www.theguardian.com/australia-news/2018/jan/11/creeping-stalinism-secrecy-law-could-imprison-whistleblowers-and-journalists

41   https://www.forbes.com/sites/bruceupbin/2011/10/22/the-147-companies-that-control-everything/

42   http://www.abc.net.au/news/2011-04-28/lifestyle-diseases-the-worlds-biggest-killer/2695712

43   ibid. see 21.

44   https://www.ncbi.nlm.nih.gov/pubmed/17666008

45   https://www.statista.com/statistics/272181/world-pharmaceutical-sales-by-region/

46   https://www.timeshighereducation.com/news/martin-boehm-preparing-students-for-jobs-that-dont-exist-yet

47   TELLINGER, M. (2013) Ubuntu Contributionism: A Blueprint for Human Prosperity. South Africa: Zulu Planet Publishers

48   http://un-documents.net/enmod.htm

49   CSIRO and Australian Government, 2006, State of the Environment Report, Australian Government Printing Service.

50   Rutherfurd, I., Tsang, A., and Tan, S.K., (2007), "City people eat rivers: estimating the virtual water consumed by people in a large Australian city", in Wilson, A.L., Dehaan, R.L., Watts, R.J., Page, K.J., Bowmer, K.H., & Curtis, A. Proceedings of the 5th Australian Stream Management Conference. Australian rivers: making a difference, Charles Sturt University.

51   Hertwich E. G. et al. Environmental Impacts of Consumption and Production: Priority Products and Materials. 2010 Report. http://www.unep.fr/shared/publications/pdf/DTIx1262xPA-PriorityProductsAndMaterials_Report.pdf (accessed 3 Jun 2010).

52   http://www.abc.net.au/news/2014-02-17/fox-speciesism-the-final-frontier/5263372

53   https://www.greenbook.org/marketing-research/influentials-innovators-early-adopters

54   https://en.wikipedia.org/wiki/The_Tipping_Point

55   GLADWELL, M. (2000) The Tipping Point: How Little Things Can Make a Big Difference. US: Little Brown

56   JUNG, C.G. (1969) The Structure and Dynamics of the Psyche. Princeton University Press

57   https://en.wikipedia.org/wiki/Christiaan_Huygens

58   http://www.dailymail.co.uk/sciencetech/article-3176193/Clocks-SPEAK-Mystery-pendulum-clocks-synchronise-ticks-tocks-solved-350-years.html

59   BECK, D.E. & COWAN, C.C. (2005) Spiral Dynamics: Mastering Values, Leadership, and Change. Wiley Blackwell.

60   ibid. see 3.

61   FREEMAN, W.H. & Co. (1992) Helplessness: On Depression, Development, and Death, Reprint edition

About Clare Mann

BSc (Hons) MSc MA Post Grad Dip. C,Occ Psychol. FBPS AMAPS

Clare Mann is an Australian-based psychologist, existential psycho therapist, best-selling author, speaker, and communications trainer. She consults with people worldwide to help address the personal and social challenges of being vegan and living in a non-vegan world. She provides training to major animal rights organisations in Australia and speaks regularly at vegan and animal rights conferences, rallies and festivals.

She runs public and in-house training programs in communication, team-building and ethical leadership, and regularly appears on TV and in the press. She has authored and contributed to numerous books. One of her books, *Communicate*, has international acclaim with foreword written by US presidential advisor Doug Wead. The principles within underpin skills training she provides for vegans. She is Editor in Chief of the digital business magazine *Ethical Futures: Conversations that Matter* – that reaches businesses with the message of animal, environmental and human justice.

She is the co-founder of the Vegan Voices Smartphone App, a free 30-day video training with tools and techniques to respond to typical communication challenges faced by vegans as well as resources to support the information they share. She is co-contributor to the Sydney Vegan Club 30-Day Vegan Challenge, the books Plant Powered Women and Everyday Vegans and a regular contributor to numerous vegan magazines and podcasts. She provides face to face and online skills training to help vegans and animal advocates communicate more effectively, and animal welfare organisations collaborate for increased effectiveness.

Other Publications

Communicate: How to say what needs to be said, when it needs to be said, in the way it needs to be said: Skills based book with proven tools and techniques to make communication your strength.

The Myths of Life and the Choices We Have: Self help book with fifty exercises to expand one's notion of choice, freedom and responsibility based on Existential Philosophy.

Human Resource Development: Strategy and Tactics: Co-authored text book for leaders, managers and university professionals on applied strategic HRD.

The Ethical Futures magazine is a digital publication, championing business and thought leaders whose practices are based on ethical leadership principles.